Making the Grades

How You Can Achieve
Greater Success
With Less Stress
In School and Beyond

Frederick Hageman

Rising Crescent Publishing
P.O. Box 7703
Berkeley, CA 94707-0703

Rising Crescent Publishing
P.O. Box 7703
Berkeley, CA 94707-0703

Cover design by Frederick Hageman and Robert Marcus

Publisher's Cataloging in Publication Data
(Prepared by Quality Books Inc.)

Hageman, Frederick., 1958-
   Making the grades: how you can achieve greater success with less stress in school and beyond / Frederick Hageman.
   p. cm.
   Includes index.
   Library of Congress Card Catalog Number: 94-68681
   ISBN 0-9643040-9-0

   1. Success--Juvenile literature. 2. Study, Method of--Juvenile literature. 3. Stress management for teenagers.
4. Success. 5. Study skills. 6. Stress (Psychology). I. Title.
BJ1611.H34 1995   158
                                      QB194-1779

This book is dedicated to Paramahansa Yogananda,
for giving me all that I have and teaching me to give it away.
Words cannot express what the heart knows.

Contents

Chapter Three
Getting Results In Advance
Imagine That!

Chapter Four
Goals--If You Don't Know Where
You Are Going, How Will You Know
When You Get There?

Chapter Five
Focus--Hey, Look at That! 65

Chapter Six
State Part I: Posture 78

Chapter Seven
State Part II: Self-Talk, Reframing, and Gratitude   **92**

Chapter Eight
Putting It All Together

Chapter Nine
What to Do if It All Falls Apart   136
--Tips for Keeping You on Track

Introduction
To Parents

Kids do not become good learners;
they *become* poor learners.
Children start off naturally loving and excelling at learning--
it's what they do all day long.
Then, far too often, something happens.

When it comes to the question of what's wrong with education today, there is no shortage of opinion (especially during an election year). There are many books, many newspaper and magazine articles, many important looking people on important sounding news shows telling us that the state of education is acute and will only get worse before it gets better. We are inundated with tales of overcrowded classrooms, overburdened teachers, underfunded programs, lack of counselors, budget cuts, drugs, gangs, and violence. In fact, it seems that there are so many things wrong with the schools that, like the little boy with his finger in the dike, whenever an attempt to tackle one problem is made, another problem springs up just out of reach. Of course, concerns about these conditions are genuine, and they deserve our attention. But, ultimately, the only thing wrong with the schools today is the performance of the students.

The Only *Real* Problem in Education
However valid the above mentioned concerns are, there's not much value in dwelling on them because, in a very real sense,

they are beside the point when it comes to improving the truly important part of education--the ability of the student to *receive* an education. With all of the talk about the problems of the schools, this point often gets confused. Time and again we hear statements such as "it is every child's right to receive a quality education." This sounds good, but it is putting things exactly the wrong way around because rights have nothing to do with it. True, it is every child's right to have a quality education *provided*, but that's something different altogether. It's like in football--the quarterback's job is to deliver the ball to the receiver. But that's all that he can do. In order for the play to be successful, it's up to the receiver to catch the ball. It doesn't matter how good the blocking is, how well executed the offensive scheme, how well thrown the ball. If it is dropped by the receiver--no touchdown. It's the same in the schools. It makes no difference how well planned the lesson is, how varied, how exciting, etc. In order for education to be successful, the student must receive it. This is not a minor point. Nor, judging from the massive amounts of time and money spent discussing and trying to deal with the bleak state of the schools, is it an obvious one to many people. So let it be stated clearly: *The only real problem in education today is in the students' inability to receive an education.* I say it is the only real problem because if it is solved, you are not going to be hearing any complaining about the lack of this or that. For example, in Japan, a country noted for its educational success, class size often exceeds fifty students. Heard many complaints about the problem of overcrowding in the Japanese schools, lately?

What Won't Fix It

So, instead of worrying about the supposed myriad problems of education, let's focus on the solution to the real problem. And the solution isn't going to come from an institutional level. The solution isn't going to come from any legislation being passed, any large sums of money being thrown at the problem, or any new theories on education. It's also not going to come with the institution of dress codes, voucher systems, or longer school days/years. All of this stuff, as nice as it sounds on TV, is window dressing; since it doesn't treat the core problem, it isn't going to work because the solution is not in an institution-down, but in a student-up approach.

What Will Fix It
What *will* work, when applied on a student by student basis, is teaching the student to change the disempowering associations and beliefs that are squelching his or her success. Then, if the student is working from a positive framework, it doesn't matter what the "state of education" is, because that student will do well in school. And the purpose of this book is to teach students how to be successful, *regardless* of the situation in their school.

Of course, there are other programs designed to help kids become better students, so it would hardly seem necessary to write another one. But this program *is* different. In the other approaches, students are taught skills in areas such as memorization, organization, note-taking, studying for facts, studying for ideas, time management, etc. These are all important elements in a successful student's repertoire. Important, sure, but since the other programs dealing with these elements are rarely as effective as they could be, this book doesn't deal with them.

Why Students Don't Receive an Education
To understand why the other approaches often fail, picture the student as a bucket. Into this bucket, with all good intention, is poured the skills of time management, organization, note-taking, etc. It seems reasonable to expect the bucket to fill, but it doesn't happen. Why not? Because the bucket has been punctured by such things as a lack of a successful student identity, disempowering beliefs ("I can't get good grades," "I hate school," "I'm just not

good at taking tests," . . .), failure to devise and follow clear-cut goals, poor focus, habitually negative states, and fear of failure. So, naturally, all of this well-intentioned information just leaks out the bottom. Until these holes in the bucket are patched, all of the programs and plans to help students improve study skills and academic performance are going to prove worthless because, however well delivered they are, the students are not *receiving* them. This book contains the tools to enable the student to patch the holes in the bucket so that he or she may receive the education and be successful, *not only in school, but in whatever pursuit he or she chooses in the future.*

Why This Book is Different

The strategies and techniques presented in this book are not my invention. They are becoming quite common in the realm of self-improvement. This is because they have proven successful in many different areas, for many different people, including business people, professionals, musicians, athletes, old people, not so old people, and downright young people. Anybody, in fact, who wants to get far better results in anything can use these techniques with great success. However, *Making the Grades is* unique because my experience as a teacher has provided me the insight needed to tailor these techniques to the particular needs of students. Unlike other sources for this information, *Making the Grades* is written directly to students and uses many examples within their everyday experience. It deals with school, the most influential environment for students because it is where they spend the majority of their time, with the majority of their peers.

Small Changes Bring Great Results

It can be a frightening prospect, this notion of changing ourselves in order to succeed in a far greater way than before. It seems reasonable to believe that great results must require great changes. And, the idea of making great changes can be uncomfortable, especially if we doubt our present abilities to make or sustain these changes. But, great results don't require great changes as much as they require small, or simple changes carefully and consistently applied. The techniques in this book are small and simple, sometimes so much so that people have difficulty believing that they can lead to such an increase in successful results.

But, little things can make big differences. I remember once being in the middle of a 150-mile trip when my car suddenly developed an exciting new condition: the front wheels and steering column shook violently whenever the car hit 55 mph. It was a frightening experience, but not nearly as frightening as the prospect of paying for what I expected to be major repairs. When I got home, I took the car to my mechanic and told him what it was doing. He said it was no big deal and pointed to a little three-inch balancing weight on the rim of the left front tire. He moved the weight over just a few inches and the problem was solved. At the cost of two dollars. A lot of our problems stem from the fact that we are off balance by just a few inches!

In response to The San Francisco Chronicle's five part examination of the California State Education System, a reader wrote: "After reading the recent reports on our public schools, I am convinced that what we need is not better schools or better teachers, but better students. The present public schools do a superb job of teaching those students ready willing and able to learn. What we need is a new agency, public or private, to prepare students to succeed in our public schools before they enter or after they fail to make progress." While I do not believe that an agency along the institutional order that this gentleman referred to is going to appear any time soon, I do believe that the techniques in this book *can* serve as the needed agency in the sense that they are instrumental in a student's becoming successful.

I know these techniques work, because if they didn't, this book wouldn't be in your hands. I say without reservation that I would not have been able to see this project through had it not been for my own application of the ideas contained herein. You see, I had to do a lot of patching of my own bucket before I could be in the position to assist anyone else in patching theirs.

Chapter One

Identity--
Who Are You, Anyway?

Two Schools

Imagine a school. We'll call it School A. The facilities at School A are first-rate. The buildings are clean and well lit, heated and air-conditioned according to season. The classrooms are carpeted, and the desks are new, with all four legs flush on the floor--no wobbling. The blackboards are large and well surfaced and there are windows which open wide and close tight. The book room is packed with clean textbooks, complete with covers and all of the pages intact. The library has a wide variety of books, many of which have been published within the lifetime of the students, and there are computerized catalogs for easy access to these books. There is a computer room with thirty-six Macintoshes and six laser printers. The photo lab, ceramics room, auto shop and band room are well stocked and well maintained. The school paper is put out every Friday. For assemblies, the auditorium can seat the entire student body. The gymnasium and athletic fields are spacious, with new bleachers, and the cafeteria serves healthy food which kids actually like!

If that sounds like a dream, let's consider a nightmare. Imagine another school, School B. The facilities at School B can't quite compare to those at school A. Everyone agrees it looks like a prison. The rooms are small and poorly ventilated (unless you count broken windows.) Many of the ancient desks are broken and the blackboards are in need of repair. The book room doesn't have enough books for the students, who must either share or buy their own, but the ones it does have sometimes have covers. The library doesn't have a large number of books either, and most of them are older than the kids. The one computer in the school is in the attendance office, but it doesn't work that well or that often. Tales of actual labs and shops are sometimes heard, but these facilities are generally regarded to have disappeared back when students stopped walking uphill both ways in the July snow. There is no school paper because of a lack of equipment and interest. There is no auditorium, so if there is an assembly, it must be held twice so that all of the students can be seated on the remaining unbroken bleachers in the gym. The cafeteria serves something like food, but there is a stigma attached to eating it, since anyone who has an alternative to doing so acts upon it.

Two Students

Now, consider two students. Student A comes to class every day, on time, with paper, pen or pencil, and the required text and assignment. Attentive when the teacher is speaking, she participates readily, offering thoughtful comments and questions. When an assignment is given, she doesn't complain, but makes sure she understands the directions and writes them, as well as the due date, in her notebook. She is well liked and is sought out regularly for help, which she gives freely and cheerfully. During study period, or if she has any free time during a class, she begins her homework and finishes it promptly when she gets home. People joke that she doesn't even have to try to maintain her straight A's, but no one really believes it. Although she is constantly busy, she always seems full of energy. No one has ever heard her complain about being tired or stressed out, but she was overheard quietly expressing concern over which university was offering her the best scholarship.

Student B, on the other hand, comes to class three or four days a week, but is often both late and unprepared. Interrupting the teacher when she arrives, she holds up class in order to tell why she was late and find someone who will give her paper and a pen. Frequently talking with both those students next to her and those across the room, she apologizes when told to be quiet and actually is for upward of a minute. During discussions, she either disparages other students' comments, makes jokes, or asks what time it is and "what time do we get out of here?"

When an assignment is given, she automatically complains that it is boring and/or stupid, and tells how another teacher has already given an assignment and she has to go to work tonight and doesn't have time for all of this work. Once she grudgingly accepts the fact that she has to do the boring and/or stupid assignment, she then lobbies to get the due date pushed back to the following week. When this fails, she asks that the assignment be repeated, but doesn't write it down because her notebook is in her locker, and, besides, she can always get it from another student.

She is always asking for help, but what she really wants is the answers, or someone to do the assignment for her. During study periods, she socializes and maintains that she doesn't have any homework or has several reasons why she can't work on it in class and will do it at home. Upon receiving her assignments back, she invariably argues that she should have received a higher grade and gets mad at the teacher, claiming she is being picked on. She often falls asleep in class because a) she is tired, b) she doesn't feel well, c) the teacher is boring, d) all of the above. She frequently tells anyone who will listen that school sucks, and that it has little to do with the "real world," which, come to think of it, she doesn't think is that great either. Generally, the rest of the class feels better when she is not there.

School Quality Doesn't Determine Student Success, Identity Does

Obviously, many people are concerned with the quality of our schools and would prefer that the school they went to, or sent their children to, was more like School A. However, the truth is that the quality of the school isn't what determines how a student will do academically. There are always kids like Student B in School A, and there are always kids like Student A in School B. Will the benefits and advantages of School A make a difference if a student is just sitting there, staring out the window? Similarly, will the disadvantages of School B stop a student from learning if that student has the determination and drive to do so? In both instances, the answer is clearly no.

Well, if it isn't the school that determines the student's academic progress, what does? Simply put, ***the most important factor in determining how a student performs is identity***. Before anything else, it is how you *see yourself* that will determine what level you perform at. Think about it. Who gets A's? You could say that smart kids do, but there are many smart kids that don't get A's. Is hard work the trick? Again, many kids who work quite hard don't get A's. The same applies to those who "kiss up." In fact, there's only one type of student who consistently gets A's, and that is an A student. Although this seems painfully obvious, it is critically important that you understand the point here. What is it about students who get A's consistently, and those who do not? As I've said, and as you know from your own classes, it's not always the smartest students, or the hardest working students who get the best grades. The students who get A's are the students who *expect* to get A's.

Expectation is the Key to Student Identity

Notice that they don't want, or merely think they deserve A's, but they *expect* to get A's. The difference between wanting something and expecting to get something is enormous, and it is this expectation that sets those students who get A's apart from the rest. It's not a matter of being conceited or thinking they are better than anyone else, either. They simply know that they are going to do the necessary work (with the necessary attitude) to get the job done. Their identity is that of an A student, so it is natural for them to get A's. *If you want to be an A student, the first, and most important step you must take is to become an A student in identity*. If you do, it will be easier for you to get A's than to not get A's. If you don't make being an A student part of your identity, you will find that you probably will not reach your goal, even if you are working harder.

This isn't about just psyching yourself up. Identity is the key for anyone who produces consistent results. And, unfortunately, it doesn't just work for producing positive results. Don't you know someone who, regardless of what he or she sets out to do, winds up reverting back to the same old person they were before they started? (Perhaps you know this person intimately?) What happens in these situations is that the person tried to make changes outwardly, but failed to make the necessary changes in *identity* that would allow those changes to stick. Therefore, they didn't expect the changes to stick. Remember, identity is the most important factor in changing the way you are behaving. If you want to have lasting change, you must first change the way you perceive yourself in that particular area.

Identity: Who are You?

Why? What is identity? The simplest way to understand identity is to begin with a question: Who are you? The easiest answer would be "I'm Joe or Judy So and so." But does this answer capture who you really are? Obviously, it doesn't, because there is so much more to a person's identity than their name. Your identity is the sum of the beliefs you have about yourself that set you apart from everyone else. It is what makes you, *you*. With a little thought, you will realize that there are many facets, or sides, to your identity.

Take a look at the different ways in which you perceive yourself. Perhaps you see yourself as an athlete, or a musician, as an actor, or an artist. Maybe you see yourself as someone who is intense, or funny, someone who is accepted, or misunderstood, someone who is basically happy, or generally sad. Do you see yourself as a winner? A loser? "I'm too thin." "I'm too fat." "I'm awkward." "I'm really good looking." "I'm ugly." "I've got it made." "I'll never get it right." These are some of the ways in which people see themselves, and it is fair to say that these labels never quite tell the whole story. As I said, we are all multifaceted people. The important thing to remember is that, along with the other aspects of your identity, you are sure to add in the fact that you are also a successful student.

We Perform According to the Guidelines of Our Identity

What is it about identity that makes it so important? Perhaps you've heard the idea that your brain is a lot like a computer. Well, in a very important sense, your brain is *exactly* like a computer: The way it runs depends on what software you put into it. What this means is that the results you get out of it depend greatly upon the expectations and beliefs (i.e., identity) that you put into it. The old computer saying, "garbage in, garbage out" applies equally well to your brain. Your brain will determine how much of your resources you will use, how hard you will work, what attitude you have, and what results you will expect in accordance with the identity you have.

Did you ever notice that those people who are always talking about how they never can do this or that, how this or that is going to go wrong, or why this or that won't work out usually wind up being right? This is because your brain will guide your experience along the lines of the way you see things. Remember, it will run the program that you load into it. If you load an identity program which tells your brain to that you are a positive, responsible person who does what is needed to get the job done, what kind of results do you think you will get? You will get results that are in accordance with your identity.

Again, this isn't merely a matter of psyching yourself up. What happens is that you start perceiving yourself as someone who behaves in a certain manner. Since that is "who you are," your ability to tap resources is shaped accordingly, as is how hard you will work, what attitude you have, and what results you will expect.

You Don't Have to "Earn" Your Identity Before You Use It

Many people believe that in order to change their identity they must first produce the results so that they are "permitted" to have the identity. Initial objections run along the lines of "How can I just change who I am? Wouldn't I be lying if I pretended to be somebody else? Wouldn't I be a hypocrite?" You don't want to fall into this type of thinking because it hampers your progress, since you will have to fight against the identity you have established as someone who doesn't "deserve" successful results yet. If you want specific results, you've got to begin by identifying yourself as the kind of person who *has* those results. Then, everything falls in line with the way you see yourself.

> If you want a quality,
> act as if you already have it.
> --William James

And don't worry. You are not going to be a hypocrite or a liar *if* you are sincere in your intention to become the kind of person who gets the results you are after. And, it should be pointed out, you don't have to go around announcing your new identity to everyone. Your new results will speak for themselves and *they* will announce your new identity. Of course, if you are just trying to fake your way through something for short term gain, you will not only be a hypocrite, but you will be a failure as well. This is not, I trust, the combination you want to pursue. You see, you cannot deceive your brain. If, on the one hand, you are meekly telling yourself, "I am an A student," but on the other hand, you are constantly undercutting this message by telling yourself, "Well, ok, not really," your brain will listen to the dominant program and guide you in that direction.

We All Want to Be Right

Identity is critical because of our inherent interest in being correct. Everybody wants to be right, don't they? This is because it's obviously a lot more fun than being wrong! Did you ever know someone who insisted they were right even when all of the evidence was clearly against them? "Don't confuse me with facts!" Or, did you ever know anyone who twisted facts in order to appear right, that no matter what angle you approach them from they will turn it towards their argument? For example, say a wife argues with her husband: "You never spend any time with me!" He insists that he does. She continues on saying "No, no. You never spend any time with me!" He then lists several instances recently where they did something together. "But you never do what *I* want to do!" "Like what?," he asks. "Well, like so on and so forth," she says. "Well, sure I do," he says and then names several instances again where he did what she wanted to do. "Yeah, but you don't *really* want to do them." And on it goes.

We all like to be correct, and our brains are no different. This is why identity is so important. If we are working from a disempowering identity, one that looks for what can go wrong, one that "knows" it can't be done, and so on, our brain will interpret events and evidence to accommodate our identity's need to be right. Similarly, if we are working from an empowering identity, one that looks for what is beneficial, one that "knows" that something *can* be done, our brain will accommodate our identity by interpreting events and evidence accordingly. After all, we all want to be right.

So, which kind of identity do you want to cultivate? Do you want to spend your time trying to prove to yourself and others that you are "right" when you say "I just can't do it." Do you want to prove to people that you can't really be expected to produce *those* kinds of results because *you* aren't that type of person? Or, do you want to get positive results because you want to prove to yourself and to others that you *are* that type of person? Remember, either direction you move in, you are going to be working to prove something in order to be correct. Which way you go is up to you.

Why Should Changing Your Identity Be So Strange?

Of course, some people are bound to think that the idea of changing their identity is a bit weird. Why this is, I do not understand. Listen folks: You *can* change your identity. You've been doing it all your life. In fact, if you didn't do it, you wouldn't be walking, or talking, or riding a bike, or reading, or writing, or any of the many things that you've learned to do which have changed the way you perceive yourself.

If you doubt that you can change your identity, just ask yourself this question: where did you get the identity you've got now? Did it come to you intact, perhaps with a wave of a magic wand? Take a closer look. It came in small installments, piece by piece. Here's how it works: Take a particular incident like forgetting an important assignment, or your backpack, or whatever. You realize what you've done and say to yourself, "I forgot it." Ok, this is not a big deal. But, if you wind up forgetting something again soon after, you may begin telling yourself that you are a forgetful person. With the repetition of a few acts of forgetfulness, you begin running an "I'm forgetful" program in your brain. Soon, every time you forget something, you go, "See, I'm forgetful." Hey--you've just created a piece of your identity. So you have to be careful that you don't acquire disempowering beliefs by turning one or two actions into disempowering notions of "the way you are." There's a big difference between "I forgot" and "I'm forgetful," between "I did poorly on that test" and "I just can't take tests."

When we start to investigate our identity, we begin to see that we are influenced by many factors. We will usually admit to being influenced by our friends, as well as TV and movies, but we might not want to admit the degree to which we are influenced by our parents. This is only natural. The day I "saw" myself sitting in a chair in the exact same way as my father did was one of the scariest days of my life! Whatever the influences, you need to keep in mind that your identity is constantly shifting according to the dominant beliefs that you hold. It's going to change, so what you want to do is *control* the direction it moves in, instead of having it shift and then accepting the changes as "the way it is" and falling in line with them because "that's the way you are."

Who Do You Want to Be?

So, to take a step in the right direction, write down who you are at this moment. Think of all of the ways to fill in the question: "Who am I?" Write down as many elements of your identity as you can think of, whether they come from physical traits, mental traits, emotional traits, achievements, whatever. Don't worry about whether they are good or bad, or right or wrong, or anything like that. Just write down as much as you can think of.

Now, think of all of the things you would like to accomplish. Without thinking about whether you could actually be that way or not, make a list of the characteristics you would need to have in order to accomplish these things and write them down. How would you need to be?

Now, look at both lists. Are there any characteristics that are on both lists? If so, these are strong elements to use for the foundation of your identity because you already have them programmed into your brain. The other elements on your second list are elements of your new identity that you will be working towards throughout this book. Please don't worry right now if you don't think you can become such a person. The truth is that at this moment, you really don't know what you can or can't do.

> If we all did the things we are capable of doing,
> we would literally astound ourselves.
> --Thomas Edison

Just focus on what you would want, and how you would need to be in order to succeed. Keep your new identity elements handy so you can have easy access to them. (In fact, it is an excellent idea for you to get a spiral notebook so that you can have all of the stuff that you do in this program in one place because you will need to refer back to things as you go on.)

As for the elements of your present identity that you don't like, just leave them aside at this time. After learning to program more empowering beliefs into your brain's computer, you will see that many of these old characteristics will just fall away because, having so much evidence to the contrary, you aren't going to believe in them anymore.

So, now that you understand that you need to change your identity in order to change your results, we need to examine the building blocks of both your identity and the results you get-- beliefs.

Chapter Two

Belief

One person with a belief,
is equal to the force of ninety-nine who have only interests.
--John Stuart Mill

Think of identity as a building. Beliefs are the bricks that it is built with. We all know we have beliefs, but beyond that we don't really think much about them. Nonetheless, beliefs are incredibly important in our lives. In fact, when it comes to shaping our lives they are more important than virtually anything else.

What Happens Isn't as Important
as the Meaning You Give It

This importance can be seen in the following illustration. Two kids grew up in a housing project in a violent, crime-ridden neighborhood. One of them, Earl, fell in step with his environment and, as soon as he was old enough, became involved in a gang and in using and selling drugs. School was not a priority, and Earl wouldn't have bothered going if it hadn't been a valuable source of business prospects, as well as a place to get into fights, and other fun stuff. As he got older, he obtained higher status in the gang and, instead of dealing drugs to friends and other students, he began dealing in larger amounts and controlling the business of other, small-time dealers.

As a lieutenant of the gang, he was arrested for the brutal attempted murder of another gang's leader. He was twenty-two years old. During questioning, he admitted he had been the one who had done the beating, and was asked why he had followed the path he had. His answer was quick and bitter: "What choice did I have, growing up where I did?"

The other kid, Edward, took a different approach growing up. Instead of using school as a place of business, he had used it as a place to learn and acquire skills. Academics, athletics, and working on the school's newspaper became priorities for him, and he starred in virtually everything he did. Instead of looking to a gang for a sense of belonging and acceptance, Edward focused on teams and clubs for the same purpose. Having received a scholarship, he attended college and excelled there as well. At his graduation, he was asked what he thought the biggest influence behind his achievement was, he answered without hesitation: "The neighborhood I grew up in--I was determined to do better than that."

How is it that two kids can credit the same circumstances for creating such radically different destinies? To make sense of this, you need to realize that it isn't the events, situations, or conditions that mold our lives, but how we *interpret* them that is the key. In other words, the things that happen to us aren't nearly as important as the meaning we attach to them. And it is our beliefs that determine what meaning we give things.

> Experience is not what happens to a man.
> It is what a man does with what happens to him.
> --Aldous Huxley

We Act on Our Beliefs About Reality, Not on Reality Itself

A belief is a sense of certainty, a sense of "this is the way it is." Beliefs act as filters between us and the outside world. You see, we don't really perceive the world directly. Think about it. How do we actually experience the world? The quick answer is that we experience it through our five senses, but this isn't exactly true. Take the eyes for example. Did you know that we don't see with our eyes? It sounds crazy, but it's true. We "see" with our nervous system and our brain. Our eyes are merely the instruments that receive the light and send it to the brain by way of the nervous system. It isn't until the brain receives the sensory stimuli and gives it meaning that we can be said to be "seeing" anything. The important thing to understand here is that, as far as our response is concerned, our brain acts on our *interpretation* of the event, not the actual event in the outside world.

Think of it like this: your nervous system is like a window between the outside world and your experience of it. Since we don't "see" things with our eyes, but with our brain by way of our nervous system, everything we experience from the outside world comes through this window. Now, the thing that makes this more than a biology lesson, is that this window is colored by our beliefs. Like tinted glass, our beliefs bias, or color, everything that comes through the window.

Your Belief Directs Your Behavior

As an example, let me tell you about a student I once had. Matt was off the wall for most of the first semester of his freshman year. He was friendly, he was enthusiastic, and he was failing. He just couldn't get his priorities straight. As he started to take a nose-dive, he saw everything coming through his belief-tinted window as another reason why he would not be able to make the grade. He saw a few F's and began to see things in that light. After this, when he received an assignment, he expected to fail, or at least do rotten on it. And, of course, he was right. Because, as you should be picking up by now, it is your beliefs which determine the direction in which your behavior will go. So he failed, and so would you if you believed the way he did. The interesting thing about Matt, though, was that he got another idea during the second semester. After a few heart to heart talks, I finally got the idea through to him that he could not only pass, but that he could get an A. He didn't believe it at first, but with enough good-natured badgering from me, he began to believe, and he began to get psyched.

Matt got the idea that he wanted an A for the second semester. Not what he should do, not what he was expected to do, but what he *wanted* to do. You can imagine how that changed things. For the first time, when he received an assignment, getting an A on it was of the utmost importance. He had a goal and he was committed to achieving it. Instead of expecting to fail and doing all of the things that would insure failure, such as procrastinating or not bothering to do the assignment at all, he was determined to do it right, and right away. Also, he would ask for help whenever he didn't understand something. Now, with getting an A being so important to him, his whole outlook on school changed, and he was excited. He would ask about his grade constantly, making sure that he was maintaining it. Since he was an athlete, he turned schoolwork into a competition and translated his athletic success into academic success. Obviously, with such attention and determination to meet his goal, he did get an A. But, the lasting benefit beyond his immediate grade, was his confidence in his ability. When it came time to register for his classes the following year, instead of taking the easier English class, which he had earlier planned on doing, he decided to build upon his success and take the more challenging class.

What happened here? Matt didn't get any smarter between semesters, and I graded him in the same way I had previously. He was in the same class, with the same teacher giving the same kind of assignments. How did he go from failing to getting an A? The only difference in the picture was the *attitude* that Matt brought with him to class. His beliefs changed, and then his performance followed his beliefs. Remember, *the beliefs you have will direct the results you get*. It's a law of human behavior.

> Man is not the creature of circumstances.
> Circumstances are the creatures of men.
> --Benjamin Disraeli

A Little Belief is Stronger than an Elephant

But you know what? It's not only humans. To see just how controlling beliefs can be, consider elephants. You know elephants, the smartest animal in the jungle and all that. Well, here's how they're trained in India. When an elephant is just a baby, its master secures one of its ankles with a heavy chain fastened to a large stake in the ground. The elephant tries to go beyond the area offered by the chain, but can't. So it tugs and tugs. After repeated attempts which go nowhere, it becomes discouraged and gives up. As the elephant grows, its master switches from chains to heavy rope, and then gradually to lighter and lighter rope. By the time the elephant is fully grown, it is strong enough to knock over a house. And yet, a thin rope is all that is needed to keep it restrained. Why? Because its belief (through past experience) that it cannot free itself from its bonds chokes off its true potential and determines the results, or lack of results that it will get. Because of past difficulties, a grown elephant lets itself be restrained without making any effort at all. It just gives up.

Now you can see why it doesn't matter whether or not a belief is based in reality. If a mighty elephant believes it cannot break a rope that in reality it could snap in a second, it's absolutely right--it can't! Many of us are just like elephants. We are operating under false beliefs, beliefs formed long ago which we have allowed to shape our lives in limiting ways. Remember, it is your beliefs that control how much of your resources you will use in any given situation. Your brain will direct your behavior in the direction of your belief.

Every man takes the limits of his own field of vision
for the limits of the world.
--Arthur Schopenhauer

What Kind of Programs are You Running in Your Computer?

Let's go back to our earlier analogy of the brain being like a computer. Beliefs are like software. If you've ever worked with a computer, you know that it is the program which determines what the computer does. Hitting the same keys on the keyboard will give you very different results depending on the program you are running. Your brain is the same way--whatever program (belief) you run will determine what you get out of it.

If you are not succeeding at the moment it is because you are running disempowering or limiting programs in your computer. The constant "I can't," "I'm not smart enough," "I'm too lazy," "I'm not good enough"--these are programmed into your brain and your brain gives you the results that are in line with these beliefs. Your brain is extremely efficient; it gives you exactly what you put into it on a consistent basis. If you want new results, you have to program in new beliefs.

If you don't believe that you can get straight A's, if you're saying to yourself that this sounds good for somebody else, but you have been getting F's and C's or whatever, and you're just not good enough or smart enough, you must remember that getting the grades isn't so much a matter of being smart enough, but of getting rid of the baggage that you have programmed into your brain. Get rid of that negative baggage and replace it with the belief that you *can* do it, and you are well on your way to accomplishing your goal. Whatever program you run, that is the results you get. It's what Matt did, and it's what you can do as well. Also, like Matt, you must realize that you don't have to settle for progress in small steps. It would have been easy for Matt to work towards getting a D, since that would seem like the logical place to begin if he was failing. *But it doesn't have to work that way.* Matt didn't go for a D. He jumped from an F to an A in one step. You can make large leaps in progress as well, skipping over the "logical" steps between, *if* you adjust your beliefs and identity to the new level you wish to operate on. It *can* happen, and it *does* happen for those people who are willing to put these techniques to work.

Beliefs are Established by Conditioning

Well, now that you understand how beliefs guide you and the value of running positive programs or beliefs to get positive results, what do you do if you have a bunch of rotten beliefs programmed in? Obviously, just saying "I don't believe them" and leaving it at that isn't going to be enough, because once your beliefs are programmed in, your behavior gets wired into your nervous system.

You see, beliefs are just like anything else--they are reinforced through conditioning, or practice. And how do you learn how to do anything? Through repetition, right? Do something over and over and it becomes second nature. This is because the repetition of an action establishes pathways in your nervous system, which are called neural pathways. The more established these pathways become, the more "automatic" an action or behavior becomes. (This is how habits, both good and bad, are developed.)

If you want a perfect example of this process, untie your shoe. Really, stop reading for a second and untie your shoe. Now, tie it as quickly as you can. How long did it take? Probably three or four seconds, right? Also, you didn't have to pay close attention to what you were doing because it's something you do every day without even thinking about it. Your "shoe tying" pathway is deeply established in your nervous system.

Now, try something different. Untie your shoe again, but this time, instead of doing it the normal way, do everything the opposite way. In other words, if you normally start by wrapping the left-hand lace over the right-hand lace, do it the other way around. If you make the loop with your right hand and wrap the left-hand lace around it before pulling it through, reverse the process by making the loop with the left hand, etc. The first thing you'll notice is that this easy, everyday routine just became something you really have to concentrate on--if you can do it at all. The reason for this is simple. Even though you are doing something that is similar to the way you normally do it, the neural pathway for this new variation has not been established, so you have to pay close attention to every step of the process.

What do you think would happen if you started tying your shoes like this every day? At first, it would be clumsy and you would have to pay a lot of attention to what you were doing. But, after awhile, it would begin to feel natural. Soon, you wouldn't be thinking about it at all--it would just be the way you tied your shoes. And, you know what? The old way, the way you had been tying your shoes all these years, would feel weird and you would have to concentrate in order to do it. Your old "shoe-tying" neural pathway would become weakened through neglect and a new one would be established in its place.

Well, as you may have guessed, since I'm not concerned with teaching you new shoelace skills, this principle works with beliefs, too. And, ultimately, if you practice, it's as simple as tying your shoes.

How to Change a Belief
So, how do you change a disempowering belief into an empowering belief, one that will enable you to get the kind of results you are after?

Step One: Decide you *must* change your disempowering belief.
This is important because if you don't feel that you *must* change this belief, you won't be motivated to actually work on changing, and you will fall back into your old patterns when the novelty of

the new idea wears off. Remember, your beliefs, like your habits, are programmed into your nervous system like software. If you don't change the program, the old one will keep running. (This is what is happening when you try to change, but can't seem to help yourself from continuing to do the exact thing you set out to change.)

When you truly decide that you are going to change, you set yourself on a new path, and, with determination, can keep moving in the right direction until you have established your new belief to the point where you don't even have to think about it anymore--it's the way you are! (Remember, beliefs are the bricks you build identity with.)

Step Two: Attach great pain to the disempowering belief.

You need to understand (and *feel*) specifically, and in detail, what your old belief will cost you now and in the future if you don't change it. For example, what is the price of living under the weight of a belief that you are lazy? Or the belief that you can never do well on tests? Or the belief that you always procrastinate? Don't just say "that's bad!" Take the necessary time and write out in detail what these beliefs are doing to your life, both in school and out. What results are you going to miss out on if you keep these beliefs? What opportunities are you going to pass up? Feel what it is like to live in such a limiting way. Do you like it? Do you think you will like what five or ten years of living with these beliefs will bring you? Again, write it out in detail so you can see the results that living under the horrible weight of this limiting belief will bring you. Don't rely on your memory to do this--it will fade. Get hard evidence in writing.

Now, you might be wondering why I am asking you to make yourself feel bad on purpose, but it's beneficial to attach a lot of pain to your old belief. This sounds weird, but it makes sense. Think of it like a toothache. When you have one, it causes you a lot of suffering because it hurts all the time. When you go to the dentist and he pulls it out, that hurts too. But when he's done, you don't have that rotten tooth causing all of that pain in your head. So, the short term pain is worthwhile because it gets rid of the long term pain. It's the same with your limiting belief. Confronting where this belief is actually leading you is painful. But when it helps to pull the rotten belief out of your head, it takes away the long term suffering you would have had to put up with if you just left that rotting belief there without taking any action.

After all, none of us likes to do things that are painful, do we? Even when we are doing things that others think are painful, we are getting *some* form of pleasure out of them. In fact, you can boil down all of our actions to the fact that, in everything, we move *away* from pain and move *towards* pleasure. It's human nature, and it's how our brain works. So, if we attach a lot of pain to our old belief, we will naturally want move away from it.

Step Three: Attach great pleasure to your new, empowering belief.

If you are going to move away from your old, limiting, painful belief, you need something to move towards. Figure out what the opposite of your old belief is. If, for example, you were being limited by a belief that you are lazy, you might want to work with the new belief that you are a hard worker. Or, if you are constantly telling yourself that you procrastinate, work with the new belief that you get your work done immediately.

Once you have your new belief (and, yes, you can work with as many new beliefs as you want), take the time and write out in detail all of the benefits that you will gain by adopting this new belief and making it part of you. What results are you going to obtain if you install this belief? What opportunities are you going to go for? *Feel* what it is like to live in such an empowering way. Do you like it? Do you think you will like what five or ten years of living with this belief will bring you? Make these feelings of accomplishment as attractive as possible. Give yourself compelling reasons to move in this new and powerful direction. Don't just haphazardly think about it or write a sentence or two. This shouldn't be an assignment you resist doing. Remember, *you are creating your success*. Right here, right now!

Now, look at what you have written about your disempowering belief side by side with the stuff from your empowering belief. Which path looks more attractive to you? Which one do you want to head down? The choice really *is* yours.

Step Four: Install the new belief into your brain's computer.

The major element to this step has to do with the concept of producing your desired results in advance, and it is the subject of our next chapter.

Disempowering Beliefs Filter Out Contradictory Evidence

Before closing this chapter, however, I want to touch on a possible objection that you might have with this whole procedure. Look, it's easy to say that you are lying to yourself if you pretend to believe something about yourself before you have any evidence to back it up. But, you shouldn't worry about this. Remember, beliefs filter out everything that doesn't fit within their confines. What happens frequently is that a person laboring under the idea that they are lazy will ignore, or fail to notice, any evidence to the contrary. For example, say a student doesn't get her school work done most of the time. When asked why, she says "oh, I'm just lazy!" Now this same student happens to be a star swimmer, and she can be found working on her swimming two or three hours a day. This obvious evidence of hard work does not fit into her belief that she is lazy, so she ignores it. If she were to change her "I'm lazy" belief into "I'm a hard worker," she could then access all of this evidence and use it for her studies, or whatever.

So, maybe you aren't a star swimmer or star athlete. Still, regardless of your belief, you *do* have evidence from your life that contradicts the limitations you are placing on yourself. Face it, there are plenty of times when you don't procrastinate, times when you feel great, enjoy school, or enjoy reading or writing, or whatever. They *are* there. You've got to focus on these times. And, yet, we don't always do so.

Once, while teaching summer school, I had a student who was a perfect example of someone who wasn't seeing the possibilities of what she could do. Now, on the first day of class, I give out a questionnaire which asks a bunch of questions to help me get to know some stuff about my new students. One of the more important questions is "What do you hate about English class?" Well, this student said that she hated everything about English class, especially writing. So, guess what she did during every free moment in class? You might think that she talked to her classmates, but that wasn't it. She spent her whole time writing letters to her friends! Since I hadn't assigned it, she didn't consider it "writing" because she enjoyed it and could write whatever she wanted. The point is, you almost always have evidence or experience to support your new belief. It's just that you've been focusing on the support for your old belief.

Create Evidence for Your New Belief

Let's say you don't have any support for your new belief. Does this mean you cannot develop it and are only lying to yourself? Yes, I'm afraid it does. Put down the book because there's nothing that can be done for you. Ok, I'm just kidding. Certainly, you can develop your new belief. All you have to do is go out and get some evidence right now. For example, if you have a new belief that you are a hard worker, go do some work and do it well. When you finish, you can say to yourself, "see, I *am* a hard worker!" It sounds like I am joking, but I'm not. If you have evidence that you can work hard and are willing to work at conditioning your new belief, you will be on your way to establishing a new belief. Just like that. The important thing to remember is that yesterday doesn't make any difference--*if* you are getting results today. Usually, however, we aren't willing to give ourselves a chance because we get stuck in dwelling on what we have been doing or not doing in the past, and this isn't always right.

Tomorrow is Not a Slave to Yesterday

As an example, say I've been smoking cigarettes and decide to quit. No matter how long I've been smoking, the day I quit, I am no longer a smoker, even if I've been smoking for twenty years before that. If I were to tell someone that I'd quit and they said, "no you haven't, you've been smoking for twenty years," it would be pretty stupid for me to say, "I guess they're right, I'm just lying to myself. I guess I'll always be a smoker." But that's what we do to ourselves if we say we can't be hard workers, or get our work done on time, or do well on tests, or whatever, if we haven't been doing so up to this point. If you truly decide to change and work to program in your new belief, yesterday is absolutely beside the point.

What you can or cannot do is determined largely by your beliefs. When you think something cannot be done, you're right-- it cannot. But, when you think it can, your belief drives you to use your resources to a far greater extent, and things that may have seemed impossible become possible indeed.

> Think you can or think you can't.
> Either way you are right.
> --Henry Ford

An excellent example of the impossible becoming possible through belief is the story of Roger Bannister. It was 1954, and for all of the years that people had been timing runners, it was believed that no one would ever be able to run the mile in under four minutes. In fact, the standard medical opinion was that it was physically impossible. But, Roger Bannister wanted to do it anyway. So, he trained intensively, believing all the while that it *could* be done. And, of course, he did do it. Such is the power of belief. But, an even more impressive testimony to the power of belief soon followed. This barrier of the four-minute mile, a barrier which had stood for so long and was seen as an impossibility, was broken by over *fifty* other runners in the following eighteen months. All because one determined runner believed that it wasn't impossible after all. Other runners saw a man achieve the "impossible," so they installed the new belief that they could do it as well. And they were right.

> Man is what he believes.
> --Anton Chekhov

Chapter Three

Getting Results in Advance-- Imagine That!

If one advances confidently in the direction of his dreams,
and endeavors to live the life that he has imagined,
he will meet with a success unexpected in common hours.
--Henry David Thoreau

In the last chapter, I said that step four for our formula for changing disempowering beliefs was to install your new, empowering belief by working to achieve the results of your new belief in advance. If you will remember, this concept was mentioned briefly in our discussion of identity, and, since beliefs are the bricks of identity, what works for identity will work for beliefs as well. And, as you will see in a later chapter, it will work with achieving goals.

Imaging is a Mark of Successful People in All Fields

There is a point you need to understand: *Success is not an accident!* There are definite qualities that foster success, and one trait that successful people in *all* fields share, is the ability to *see* themselves achieving their goals *before* they set out to achieve them, of getting results in advance. This concept is known by various names: visualization, mental scripting, mental rehearsal, mental mapping, imaging, and so on. Whatever the name, it is the same principle. (I'll be using the term "imaging" here.) If you want to be a successful student (and I'm sure you do, or you wouldn't have read this far), you will be moving yourself a great way along your path if you develop the habit of imaging in advance the results you are trying to achieve.

Your Brain Responds to a Strongly Imagined Idea as if It Were Real

One of the main reasons this works is that the brain responds to strongly imagined ideas and then moves in the direction that they provide. Think of when you're falling asleep at night. Have you ever had the experience of being in that state between sleeping and waking when you start having those weird dreams? What happens when you dream of, say, somebody throwing something at you? Your arm flinches, or your head jerks while you are laying in bed, and you wake up. Why does this happen? Because your brain can't tell the difference between reality and imagination--if the imagination is strong enough. Remember Roger Bannister? His achievement, and its effect on other runners, is an inspiring testimony to the power of belief. But there's more to the story. Bannister knew that in order to attain his goal, he would have to train as hard mentally as he did physically. One of the things he did was run the race in his mind, step by step, finishing the race in under four minutes. He did this constantly, and it prepared his mind to accept the possibility of doing it during the actual race. When you strongly imagine something, your brain takes this as an indication of the direction you want to move in, and it begins moving you in that direction.

Of course, Bannister isn't the only athlete to have worked on visualizing results. Athletes from all sports routinely go through this process. It is an important part of their training. Superstar athletes such as body builder, Arnold Schwarzenegger; gymnast, Mary Lou Retton; decathlon champ, Bruce Jenner; golfer, Jack Nicklaus; and Bill Russell, center on *eleven* Boston Celtic NBA championship teams, have all used imaging as a central part of their training. Barry Bonds, of the San Francisco Giants, has said that in order to prepare himself for next game, he visualizes the opposing pitcher's delivery and what he will need to do in order to have a successful at bat against that pitcher. And, as most baseball fans know, Barry Bonds is considered by many to be the best player in the game today.

We All Image,
But Most People Work for Negative Results

Now, if this stuff just worked for athletes, there wouldn't be much point in bringing it up here, would there? But remember, a key trait of successful people in *all* fields is their ability to see their results in advance. By conditioning their mind in this way, they reach the point where they *expect* to succeed.

This expectation makes all of the difference. But, sadly, most people expect to *fail* in most situations, and spend much of their mental energy going over and over their fears and expectations of this failure. When they eventually do fail, their response is along the lines of "see, I knew it!" I see this happen with students all the time. Before a test or an essay, they quietly (and sometimes not so quietly) whip themselves into a state of mind which allows them little chance of success because it is totally focused on failure. And they *do* fail.

Well, of course they do--look at what's going on here. They've become experts at exactly what I'm talking about in this chapter. They're getting results in advance, but they're getting rotten results!

> The thing always happens that you believe in;
> and the belief in a thing makes it happen.
> --Frank Lloyd Wright

Say you are one of these students who habitually expects to do poorly. What if you were to use the *same habit that you already have*, but, instead of using it to get negative results, you used it to produce positive results? You *can* do this, you know. There's no rule that says you have to always expect to do poorly, even if you have done so up to this point. Past failures are like mud you've walked through, and the present is like a new white carpet. And, hey, nobody wants you bringing your muddy boots on this beautiful carpet, so take them off!

Stop Being So "Realistic"

Now, for all of you people who will insist that you're "just being realistic" about your abilities, I've got a question. Why is it that every single time, without exception, that somebody is "just being realistic," they are being negative, or in some way trying to excuse why something can't be done? Why is it that "being realistic" is never positive? Why is it that "being realistic" always seems to be an effort to put the brakes on some kind of progress?

Take a look around you at all of the everyday items that we take for granted, the cars, the planes, the televisions, the telephones, and so on. Not a single one of these inventions, along with countless others, was "realistic" at the time they were being worked on. And you can be sure that every step of the way there was someone whispering in the ear of the inventors, trying to talk them out of what they were doing, all the time saying they were "just being realistic." As an example of how limiting this "realistic" talk can be, think of the toilet. Can you believe that when it was first being developed and introduced that there were many people who were "just being realistic" when they pointed out that it would be an insane idea to think that people would actually want something like a *toilet* in their house? After all, that was something you took care of outside, away from where you lived!

Another thing about these inventions and everything else that you see out there in the "real" world is that there isn't *anything* that's been built or invented or created or whatever that hasn't first been *imagined* in the mind. Everything comes from the mind--which is why you shouldn't worry so much about the "real" world. After all, the majority of your life doesn't take place there, anyway. It takes place between your ears, and what you are consistently doing *in there* determines what will happen on the outside, because your beliefs filter your experience of what's "real." So, forget about being 'realistic!' It's just a code word for limiting beliefs when it's used in this way.

> What is now proved was once only imagined.
> --William Blake

In Which Direction are You Going?

Whether you succeed or whether you fail is determined by how you spend your mental time. We're always thinking about something, and our thoughts generally fall into habitual patterns. As I said, successful people expect successful results, and spend much of their mental effort imaging successful results in advance. They're using the *same technique* that unsuccessful people are using, but they're pointing it in a positive direction instead of a negative one. That's why positive imaging is such a wonderful practice. When you do it consistently, with concentration and deep feeling, the message that is sent to your brain is "I'm doing it now, so I will be able to do it later, as well." Since you are going to be imaging anyway, whether you do it positively or negatively, in which direction do you want your mental effort to point?

> Losers visualize the penalties of failure.
> Winners visualize the rewards of success.
> --Dr. Robert Gilbert

The Four Steps for Changing a Belief (in Review)

So how do you practice imaging when it comes to your new belief? Before we go into that, let's quickly review the first three steps of changing your disempowering belief.

The first step was to determine what belief you wanted to get rid of and decide, once and for all, that you weren't going to be ruled by this belief anymore. Remember, without this determination, you risk falling back into the old belief due to the fact that it is already programmed into your brain.

The second step was to attach lots of pain to your old belief. This is necessary because you move *away* from pain and *towards* pleasure. If you feel that your old belief and the results it brings you are painful, then you will naturally want to move away from it.

The third step was to determine your new, empowering belief and attach a lot of pleasure to it. This is necessary because you need something to move towards while you are moving away from your old belief. By attaching a lot of pleasure to the new belief and the results it will bring, you give your brain a reason to move in that direction.

The fourth step is to begin programming your new belief into your brain. I said that it was important to find evidence to back up your new belief from past experience, and, if that wasn't possible, to go out and get some evidence in the present. And, of course, you will want to practice imaging, or getting results in advance.

The Imaging Routine

Let's work through an example to see how this works. Say you've been having trouble getting your work done, or you do it, but you don't put much effort into it. If this is a normal situation for you, you are probably running some variation of the belief program, "I'm not a very good worker because I'm lazy." This belief gets you the kinds of results that you'd rather not brag about. A good belief to use instead of this disempowering belief is "I am a hard worker who gets the job done." (I needed to program this one for myself in order to get over a major belief of being lazy, a belief which was habitually holding me back from getting any serious work done and had hurt me for years. If you want physical proof that these techniques really work, look no further than this book you are holding in your hands. I could never have seen this project through if it weren't for the tools that I am teaching you right here.)

Preliminary Imaging Points

Before we go through the example, let's go through some points that will help you get the most out of your imaging practice.

First, you need to find a quiet place where you can work without being bothered for at least five or ten minutes. This is important because it is necessary to concentrate on what you are doing without worrying about being interrupted or disturbed. The deeper you can get into your imaging, the more effective your practice will be.

You need to be comfortable and in a position where you can relax. Lying down is ok, but many people find it too easy to drift off to sleep. If this presents a problem for you, try sitting in a comfortable chair. Close your eyes and take a few slow, deep breaths until you are feeling calm. The greater the state of relaxation you can get into, the better your results will be.

When you do your imaging work, try to make it as complete as possible, filling in as many details as you can from the surroundings you are placing yourself in, and feeling as strongly as you can the benefits you are seeking. For example, if you are working on a situation for a certain class, see yourself in that classroom as best you can. Get *excited* about the results you are imaging because the more intensely you can feel them, the more they will manifest in your real class. This may seem difficult at first, but, as you practice, you will get better. The more "real" you can make your imaging, the more your brain will be compelled to move you in that direction because, as far as it is concerned, you *are* moving in that direction.

A Hard Working Example

Now that you have taken care of the preliminaries, take your new belief (In this example, "I am a hard worker who gets the job done.") and think of a situation where it would apply. For example, imagine a type of assignment that you are likely to receive, one that has caused you difficulty in the past. Put yourself in the position of getting that assignment. Are you going to be like most students? Are you going to approach it with resistance and the expectation of struggling through it, miserable and whining about how mean the teacher is for giving it? *No*. You're a hard worker, and hard workers attack their assignments with enthusiasm; they don't waste their time and energy trying to get out of doing it. (Like I said earlier, this is why they always seem to be half finished when the others are just getting started.)

See yourself in your imagination starting your assignment immediately after receiving it. No resisting, no complaining, you just do it. Feel that wonderful feeling that comes from knowing that you are again about to successfully accomplish something. See yourself working hard to finish your task. See yourself working steadily; you're not rushing just to get it done. Feel how good it feels knowing that you attacked it with gusto and put in the necessary effort to do a great job. Feel the confidence that comes from such an effort, confidence that you can apply to any area you choose because hard work in one area translates to hard work in other areas as well. After all, you *are* a hard worker. See yourself getting an A on the assignment. Feel how good it is to be getting A's consistently. See yourself bringing home a report card with straight A's. How does it feel to hand a report card like this to your mom or your dad? How does it feel to have them be so proud of you? How does it feel to know that your hard work has brought you yet another success? How does it feel for *you* to be proud of you? Feel these positive feelings deeply. The success and pride that come along with these feelings are the result of the fact that *you* are a hard worker who gets the job done.

Repeat this process daily for a couple of minutes, using different situations and emphasizing the fact that you are a hard worker who gets the job done (or whatever belief you are working with) and feeling how good it feels to be accomplishing so much more than you were before. Before you go to bed or when you get up are both excellent times to work on this, but you can do it anytime you have a few minutes to spare. The more you do it the better you get at it, and the better you get at it, the better your results. And, remember, the more intensely you can *feel* the results, the more you can tie them to positive emotions, the deeper they will go into your brain.

> Dreams have as much influence as actions.
> --Stephane Mallarme

Imaging Plants Seeds of Success

Remember, repeating an action over and over again sets up neural pathways in your nervous system, just like I talked about in the shoe-tying example. And, as I said, your brain doesn't know the difference between your doing something for real and your strongly imagining yourself doing something. So, if you work with concentration and feeling (just like so many great athletes and other professionals do), you are mentally training. This mental repetition will greatly assist you in your actual acquisition of the skills or beliefs that you want to achieve.

Imaging, or getting results in advance is like planting seeds-- you are going to harvest what you plant. By planting positive, deliberate images of your success in your mind, you are preparing yourself for a successful harvest. Of course, this isn't magic--you still have to do the work along the way, just as you do when you plant a garden. But, if you are consistently working on your belief in your imagination, you will see that you are getting similar results in real life, and you will start thinking of yourself in terms of your new belief.

This identification with your new belief will lead you to get better at your imaging, and that in turn will make you *want* to work towards achieving the same results for real because you will know how good it feels to be successful and in control of the direction in which your life is going. Getting results is a lot more fun than sitting around complaining about how you're bored, or how much school sucks, or whatever. As you build up momentum, you will get more and more evidence for your new belief. Soon, you won't have to consciously work on it because it will be a stable part of who you are. Imagine how good that feels!

> One's life is dyed in the color of his imagination.
> --Marcus Aurelius

Chapter Four

Goals--
If You Don't Know Where
You Are Going, How Will You
Know When You Get There?

Imaging is a wonderful technique to help you condition your new beliefs, and it is also a great way to help you condition your identity to fall in line with the kinds of results you want to achieve. But what results do you want to achieve? "Well, that's easy. I want to get better grades. I want to be a better student." These are good things to want, but they're a little vague, aren't they? In order to help you get better results faster, we need to spend some time with another trait that successful people of all stripes share: the ability to set specific goals.

Everything that has been created by anyone--any invention, building, work of art, symphony, bridge, organization, or whatever, has started out in the imagination as a dream and, therefore, had to be a goal before it came into physical being as a successful achievement. If you are serious about being successful in your schoolwork or any other pursuit you are interested in, you must understand the power of goal setting.

However necessary goals are to success, they do seem to frighten a lot of folks, and many people will purposely keep their dreams vague. It's as if they think they might sneak up on these dreams and get lucky, or that they can sneak away quietly without any real commitment if things don't work out. But this haphazard approach to success is *not* the approach that you want to take. Remember: *Success is not an accident!* If you want to succeed, you need to plan for it because if you don't, you're planning for something else.

Failing to plan
is planning to fail.

Goals Can Carry You Through Failures and Keep You on Track

One of the most common objections to setting definite goals is "what if I set a goal and then fail to achieve it? Aren't I setting myself up to be disappointed?" It's true that there is risk involved, but, hey, there's always risk involved in any achievement, isn't there?

One doesn't discover new lands without consenting
to lose sight of the shore for a very long time.
--Andre Gide

We all like security. But in order to reach new heights, we've got to take some risks. It's like in baseball: You can't steal second with one foot on first. Unless you're willing to never try anything at all ever again, you are going to have to take some chances. And some of these chances are not going to work out. Well, so what? Nobody succeeds without failing a lot along the way. The difference between the winner and the loser is that the winner gets up and keeps on going, while the loser stays down and quits. It's not falling down you want to worry about, but whether or not you get back up. And, goals give you a reason to get up again.

Another great thing about goals is their ability to keep you on track. Without goals you can wander aimlessly for years, never knowing where you are going, or what's around the next corner. As bad as that sounds, it's normal. Wandering around is the way the great majority of people spend their lives. And, if you look around, you can see that most people are not satisfied with the quality of the life they're living. Are you?

A Valuable Study of Goals

If you are skeptical about the value of specific goals, think about this. There was a study done at Yale University in 1953 concerning goals. They surveyed the graduating class and found that only 3% of the students had specific, written goals and a plan to achieve them. The rest of the class had only vague plans of being in business, or being a doctor, lawyer, architect, teacher, or whatever. Twenty years later, in 1973, they did a follow up study to see how the class of '53 had fared. Happiness and fulfillment are pretty subjective concepts, and are difficult to measure. Still, it did seem to the researchers that the students who had the written goals had generally been quite a bit more successful in these areas than those students without the written goals. But, in a more concrete, objectively verifiable category of success, the results were truly remarkable: The 3% who had specific, detailed goals with written plans of action were worth more in financial terms than the other 97% combined! Clearly defined goals are *essential* to your success and achievement.

We All Have Goals,
But Where are They Leading Us?

Although I'm putting special emphasis on goals at this point, I'm not implying that they are something brand new for you to learn about; they are already a regular part of everyone's life. After all, we're all chasing something, aren't we? No matter what we are doing, we are trying to achieve a specific end. Even the student who just sits there every day staring into space or sleeping is pursuing something, even if it's just a way of getting through the day without having to do anything or be bothered by anybody. But these short term goals are not the same as the specific, long-range goals you want to learn to develop. Like everything else in this book, it's a matter of learning to use the skills you *already have* in a more positively focused way, of taking conscious control of these skills that you've been using unconsciously all along.

Goals Let You See Past Distractions and Obstacles

The difference between the chronic failure and the successful person is that the failure has only short-range goals which are easily set aside whenever any old whim comes along, while the successful person has long-range, specific goals which carry him or her through distractions and problems. [I'm just now putting the final touches on the editing of this book before it goes to print, which means that, what with writing, revising and editing, I've read through it what seems like at least fifty-seven times, and it strikes me how may things have gone wrong along the way, the problems that have arisen, the delays and the headaches they have caused. But never have I looked at it as failing. It's all part of the process. Just keep going, folks.]

You see, goals drive your actions. When you have a definite, specific direction in which you are moving, you are able to see past temporary obstacles by keeping your eyes on your goal. Without goals, every little problem that comes up can affect you greatly because, without the long-range vision that goals provide, the problem is all that you can see.

For example, as a student, there are going to be times when you will not like either the subject, the class, or the teacher. This is just the way it goes. Now, what happens to most students in this situation is that they get sidetracked by this dislike and do poorly in the class. If you ask them why they do horribly, they are quick to tell you that they hate English or math or biology, or their horrible, boring, ugly, stupid, smelly, fat, old, cranky, kid-hating teacher who, for no reason whatsoever (since they never did anything wrong), hates them and treats them unfairly. What happens is that, since they have no specific goal that they are working towards, they let any obstacle block their way because that's as far as they can see.

But it isn't that way with students who have clear-cut goals because they approach things differently. Instead of getting bogged down in whether or not he likes the teacher or subject or class, the goal-oriented student focuses on the task at hand and doesn't let these other factors distract him. Maybe he thinks the subject is boring, or the teacher is boring or mean or stupid or whatever. It doesn't matter because all of these things are beside the point. The goal-oriented student knows that long after the class is over the grade will remain, so he keeps his mind on the goal of getting the A and moves on, whether he likes the situation or not.

The View From Both Sides of the Fence

I have to admit that I learned this idea the hard way. All throughout high school, I was the classic complainer about how dumb my classes were, not to mention the stupidity of the fact that I had to spend so much time dealing with things that I was never going to use in my life, ever. Needless to say, I was a rotten student, and my report cards reflected the fact. (I never had an A, got maybe one or two B's, and the rest of my grades were C's, D's, and F's.) When I graduated, I had no direction and no plans of going to college. But, after eight years of dead end jobs, frustration, and feeling like a total loser, I finally decided to go back to school at the age of twenty-six. Desperately intent on making up for lost time, I had a different attitude altogether. I also had a definite goal--I was determined to get straight A's. It took me three semesters to finally achieve my goal, but once I did, I continued to get straight A's the rest of the way, graduating with top honors. (Talk about changing your identity!) And one of the biggest factors in my success was realizing that my feelings about the class or teacher or whatever had *nothing* to do with my performance or my determination to achieve my goal. (And believe me, nothing you have experienced could possibly prepare you for the mind-numbing boredom of education classes.) Goals help you get past the distractions.

Goals Help to Keep You Motivated

Let's face it: Just because you have a specific direction you are heading in and you have a workable plan to achieve it, doesn't mean that every step of the way is going to be easy. Or fun. Without goals, people get sidetracked easily whenever their initial inspiration wears off (and it always does!) You know from anything you've ever accomplished, whether it be a sport or musical activity or whatever you might have done, that sometimes it's not as fun or exciting as other times. This is natural, so you basically have two choices: quit or go on. People without specific goals generally quit and move from whim to whim, never sticking with anything and wondering why they're unhappy. (They also spend a lot of time putting down other people who are accomplishing something.)

But, people with specific goals find that having a definite direction to move in allows them to focus on the ultimate result and push through the difficult times, the times when they just don't want to do it (whatever it is). By seeing the big picture and the ultimate reward, you can keep your excitement level higher and take greater steps towards your goal. And, the great thing about this is that every little victory or accomplishment along the way fuels you with more excitement, which in turn drives you to accomplish more. It's called an upward spiral of achievement, and it feels incredible.

Goals Make Hard Work Fun

Also, when you have a specific goal you are working on, it makes working hard not only easier, but, believe it or not, it makes it fun. Like I said before, accomplishing things is much more fun than sitting around complaining about being bored or whatever. And pursuing a goal makes you **want** to excel, which lets you tap resources that you might not believe you had, or wouldn't have used if you hadn't been focusing on your goal.

A while back, I had an experience which perfectly illustrated the truth of this last point in a way that will stay with me forever. I'm a hiker. While investigating a new trail one day, I found a mountaintop that overlooked the Pacific ocean and the surrounding forests and valleys of Point Reyes National Seashore in Marin County, California. It was the highest point in the park, and it seemed to me to be a perfect place to see the sunrise. The only problem was that it would be impossible to reach by the way I had come because I would have to start out at least two and a half hours before dawn, and there's no way I could walk the trails in total darkness. But the trail that I took back to the trailhead was shorter than the approach trail. It was so steep, however, that I hadn't even considered going up that way. But, when I got the idea of reaching the top of the mountain before the sun broke the horizon, things changed.

Now I had a specific goal, and I got excited about achieving it. Returning to the park before dawn the next weekend, I was determined to beat the sun, which was to rise at 5:49 that day. It was 5:15 when I arrived, so I had thirty-four minutes to make the two-mile journey uphill to the peak. This was something that I normally would not have been able to do on a grueling trail like this one. But, now that I had my goal, I was driven to succeed--I **had** to reach the top of the mountain before the sun broke the horizon, so I was psyched. I can honestly say that I have never worked so hard at anything in my life. I surpassed every limit I had had for pushing myself and just powered up that trail. Even though my legs were killing me and I was short of breath, the idea of succeeding felt so good that it overpowered any idea of stopping or slowing down.

Well, I made it with four minutes to spare, and the feeling of victory was indescribable. I had performed at a level far beyond any that I had ever experienced before. Now, what was it that allowed me to perform at this higher level? If I was just hiking up this trail, I wouldn't have worked nearly as hard. But, because I had a specific goal of beating the sunrise, it gave me a focus and determination to achieve results beyond what I was normally accustomed to producing--it opened a channel into deeper resources that I had never used before, resources that I didn't even know I possessed. Also, it made working hard exciting and fun.

> Deep within man dwell those slumbering powers;
> powers that would astonish him,
> that he never dreamed of possessing;
> forces that would revolutionize his life if aroused
> and put into action.
> --Orison Swett Marden

The Size of the Goal is Not the Important Thing

We tend to think that only large-scale accomplishments or big situations can be major victories. This isn't true. The preceding example had a major impact on me, but it wasn't a major incident in the grand scheme of things. After all, it *was* just a hike, however rigorous. But the lesson that it taught cut deep within me. Now, when I get in a situation where I don't think I can do something, whether big or small, I remember that race to beat the sunrise, and I know that I have the ability within me, if I will only make up my mind to do it and follow through. So remember, it's not the size of the goal that you set, it's your ability to set it and achieve it. Once you do, you can use it to reinforce your confidence and further condition your beliefs that you *are* successful. Also, success is success. If you can do it in one area of your life, you can do it in others as well, because you are using the same traits.

Goals Can Help You Break Out of
Your Comfort Zone

Another important point illustrated in the hiking incident is the idea of reaching for something beyond what you think you can do, of breaking through your comfort zone. Generally, we all like to work within a certain set of limits, a place that, because it is familiar and doesn't present us with any surprises, lets us be comfortable. This place is known as the "comfort zone," and we all have one, although some people have an easier time getting beyond theirs. (Don't let the term "comfort" fool you; the comfort zone isn't a positive place because it often chokes us off from new experiences and chances to grow.) When something comes up that is beyond our comfort zone, we tend to fear it, or reject it, or jump to conclusions as to why it won't work, or why it's impossible, or stupid, or whatever.

Many students have comfort zones that are quite rigid, and it is often difficult to get them to see past them. Every year, I meet kids who are quick to insist that they can't write very well, or they can't take tests, or they are going to do poorly on certain assignments because they're just not good at that kind of thing. Of course, these attitudes come from limiting beliefs and can be overcome by using the techniques I described earlier (in the chapter on beliefs.) One of the hardest things to do, however, is to get these students to even *attempt* to change because the very idea of doing something different, or producing new results in their area of weakness, goes beyond their comfort zone and they refuse to take any action at all. Not all cages have bars!

In situations where you become fenced in by your comfort zone, a goal can be a very effective means of pulling you through--if you make sure that it is something that goes beyond what you normally would attempt to do. This is what happened in my hiking example. I set a goal that was far beyond my comfort zone, far beyond what I normally would have attempted or what I thought I could do. And, by accomplishing it, I discovered not only how *limiting* my comfort zone was, but just how possible it was to overcome it when the need arose.

The Momentum Goals Provide
Helps You Persevere

When you get going on a goal, you start to build up momentum and the whole process becomes easier. After all, isn't getting started the hardest part of any project? And much of the reason for this is that frequently, we aren't sure where we are going, so we drag our feet. With a clear goal, we know where we are going and we can get excited about pursuing it because the uncertainty has been removed and we don't have any doubts about what we are going after.

Also, this momentum is valuable in helping you to keep going when things get difficult or start going wrong. As I said earlier, most people, since they don't have their goals in order, give up their pursuit of something when things start to get difficult. Instead of sticking it out, they run away and begin to chase after something else that looks easier. What they fail to realize is that once the novelty wears off, *anything* worth pursuing is going to involve periods where things get tough. Can you imagine a great athlete, or musician, or scientist, or business person who didn't have the perseverance to push through the tough times? I can't either, because such a person doesn't exist! Every field or pursuit has its difficulties. And, in every field, there are those who succeed and those who quit. It's the person with the clearly defined goal that becomes successful, because the goal gives that person a constant target to aim for, and the momentum that person builds up as the pursuit gets under way helps push barriers aside.

Guidelines for Setting Goals

Regardless of the goals you wish to pursue, there are a few guidelines to help you get the most out of your effort.

Step One: Write down in detail your goals and the plans for their accomplishment.

For different reasons, people generally want to skip this part. Of course, there is the resistance that students generally have to writing **anything** down! But, beyond that, there seems to be the idea that just figuring out this stuff mentally will work just as well. It won't. First of all, by being unwilling to commit your goals to writing, you are sending a message to your brain that you are not truly serious about accomplishing them. Before you object to this idea, consider the possible reasons for *not* writing down your goals. Can you honestly say that your reasons for not writing them down are not grounded in either laziness or fear? If they're not, you are a unique individual. By failing to write your goals down, you will be missing out on two advantages that will prove highly beneficial to your success: *clarity* and *permanence*.

By writing down your goals and plans, you begin to see more clearly what needs to be done in order for you to be successful. When you limit your goals to mental figuring, you are bound to leave out important details because you are so close to them, so to speak. When you write them down and stand back from them, you can see them for what they are, not what you *think* they are. Hey, have you ever taken notes during a class and later had trouble figuring out what they were about? What happened was that at the time of your note-taking, you were filling in the details, or context, in your head, so what you wrote made perfect sense. Later, when the details were pushed aside by whatever you had to do next period or something else that you got involved in, the context of the notes was lost, so they weren't clear anymore.

It's the same with your goals. You are inclined to forget details that seem so clear when you initially work out your ideas. By writing them down, you not only are able to work out important details, but you also get a better picture of what you are working towards. You see, when something is in your mind, it tends to shift as time goes on. When your goals are only mental, they will start losing their clarity. As situations arise and you naturally start making adjustments to adapt, what started out as your goal will also begin to shift, and you may very easily find yourself working towards something quite different than your original plan. And usually, this "something different" turns out to be a settling for something less than what you started with. Of course, having mental goals is better than having no goals at all, but if you're serious about accomplishing what you originally set out to do, be smart and write down what you are after. Then, you can review your goal and get fresh inspiration and motivation, especially when things get difficult, which they certainly will at some point. (Trust me.)

As soon as you realize the goal that you want to pursue, begin writing a preliminary plan for achieving it. This plan does two things for you. It makes your goal that much more real to your mind when you have some sort of plan to achieve it, and it helps you to organize your resources and strategies in a way that you can review consistently. Writing things down forces you to concentrate more on what you are doing, and it also quickly shows you how vague your ideas can be. Often, people think that they know just what they are after, but when they try to write their goals and plans down, they realize that they can't get a clear handle on what they are doing. It's a very efficient test: If you can't write it down in a clear manner, you haven't thought it through enough. This *doesn't* mean that you need to have every detail of your plan firmly in place before you begin, but it does mean that you need to know what you are going after. When writing your plan, consider these questions regarding your goal:

❒ What will you need to achieve your goal?

❒ What resources do you already have to help you? (Think! There are always more than you realize at first.)

❒ Who can you find to help you achieve your goal--friends, family, teachers, administrators? Now, you might think that teachers and administrators would be too busy, or not want to help you. But, for the most part, this is not true. If a teacher or administrator sees a student who is determined to succeed, they will usually bend over backwards to help that student. Even if you haven't had the best relationship with them beforehand, if they see you are sincere and want to make things better, you will receive the necessary help. Most people, even teachers and administrators, would rather have positive interactions with you than negative ones. Honest!

❐ Who do you know who is already getting the results that you want?

❐ What are they doing to get these results, and how can you do the same? This concept is called *modeling* and it is extremely valuable. Please take the effort to find some models because you will save a lot of time and effort in the long run. Again, you might think that someone would not be willing to help you become successful, but you would be surprised. If you approach someone sincerely with the idea of modeling them, they will generally be glad to help you. Think about it. You are telling them that you want to be like them. People love to share their success with other people. It gives them validation that they *are* successful.

❐ How much time will you need to work on your goal daily/weekly?

❐ What is standing in the way of your success, and how can you remove that obstacle?

❐ What kind of skills will you need in order to achieve your goal?

❐ What kind of characteristics will you need in order to achieve your goal? This involves the type of person you need to be--your identity. (By now, I'm sure you are seeing how all of this stuff works together.)

Write the answers down. The more details you can come up with, the better off you will be because the clearer the picture your brain has, the more compelled it will be to move in the direction of your goal.

Of course, writing down your goals does not mean that you are locked into them if you realize that changes in your plan are necessary. Sometimes, as you move along in your pursuit, you see things that you didn't consider initially. Fine. Make the necessary adjustments and keep on working.

Step Two: State your goal in the positive.

You don't want goals that merely move you away from negative situations, but ones that move you towards positive ones. Of course, getting away from negative situations is a good start, but it's not a fulfilling place to stop. Nor will it take you as far as you ultimately want to go. For example, say you set a goal of no longer failing math. What you have here is a goal stating what you don't want--to fail math. It's not a bad idea, not failing math, but it has its problems as a goal. For one thing, you wouldn't want to limit yourself to just passing math if, using the same amount of effort, you could do much better by being more focused and positive. Remember, the motivation for achieving a goal comes in part from the excitement generated by the goal itself. Which accomplishment would make you happier (and, therefore, excited)--getting a D in a subject you had previously failed, or getting an A? Which goal do you think is going to drive you towards using resources that you don't normally use? (And, yes, it *is* possible to make large leaps in progress like going from F's to A's. Remember Matt? See p. 20.)

Also, if you have a goal that is stated in the negative, you are spending much of the time focusing on what you don't want. For instance, say that you design a goal that is stated, "I will no longer procrastinate when it comes time to do my homework." Now, as you will learn in the upcoming chapter on *focus*, you tend to get what you pay attention to. Even though you don't want to procrastinate any longer, your attention, as dictated by the language of your goal, is still on procrastination. So, it is better to state your goal in the positive: "I will do my assignments as soon as I get home from school." (Or whatever your goal is.)

Then, you are putting your attention on what you want, instead of on what you don't want. As another example, instead of stating your goal, "I will not get angry whenever such and such happens," state it in the positive: "I will stay calm whenever such and such happens." It seems like a small difference, but with the first, your mind is still focusing on anger, the thing you want to get rid of, while in the second, your mind is focusing on calmness, the thing you want. This is the better way to go because it allows all parts of your mind to move in the same direction, thereby improving your prospects of succeeding.

Step Three: Make sure your goal is something *you* can control.

You want to be sure that what you are after is something that is within *your* domain. It shouldn't be dependent on someone else in order for it to be accomplished. For example, goals like "my friends won't bother me when it is time to study," or "my algebra teacher will not be so mean to me" are *not* within your control because other people have to do certain things in order for your goal to be accomplished. You only want to have to pay attention to *your* performance, not someone else's. Often, these goals can be reworded so that they will still accomplish the same objective, but with *you* as the main focus, instead of someone else. For example, "I will not be distracted when it comes time to study" accomplishes the same objective as "my friends won't bother me when it's time to study," but it puts *you* in control. "I will not give my algebra teacher any reason to be mean to me" puts you in control of your objective. Of course, there's no guarantee that your algebra teacher won't be mean to you, but at least *you* are behaving properly. Having a cranky algebra teacher may just be your lot in life. But, if your goal puts you in control of obtaining your objective, at least you won't be putting yourself in the line of fire as often! You will just get your A and move on.

Step Four: Be sure you can tell
when you have accomplished your goal.

This is such an important point. You need to know when you have been successful. It sounds funny, but often, people set goals that are so vague that they never appreciate the progress they make. This is why you don't want to set goals like "I will be a better student," or "I will work harder in Spanish." How will you know when you are getting "better" or working "harder," when you are doing "good" or "great," or when you are "improving"? All of these descriptions are too vague; you need to be specific enough in your goal to have clear evidence of your success. To be sure that you are doing this when you make your goals, just ask yourself the question: "How will I know when I've accomplished my goal?" If you can answer the question easily, then you know that your goal is specific enough. If not, reword it so that you can tell when you have succeeded.

Something that frequently happens when we start working on goals is that we tend to lose sight of our achievements because when we improve at something, we are inclined to take for granted what once was quite an accomplishment.

For example, not long ago, I started running every day. Initially, there was a certain hill that I always walked up because it was too hard to run up. (Oh, no--another hill story!) One day, as I started my run, I was considering trying to run up the hill, but I wasn't too serious about it. When I got there, there was this guy who was about twenty years or so older than me, running towards the hill from another direction. So, I said to myself, "if *he* runs up that thing, *I'm* going to do it, too!" Well, he started up it, and I followed, using him as my motivation to make it. We were both running very, very slowly, but we kept on running. By the time I started to get close to the top, I thought I was going to fall over dead. But, since *he* was doing it, *I* wasn't going to stop. Needless to say, I was very proud of myself when I made it to the top because I had pushed myself hard and accomplished a specific goal that I had set for myself.

Since then, because I have improved in my running ability, it is no big deal for me to get to the top of that hill. But that doesn't diminish the accomplishment that I made on that day. Even though I have advanced beyond that point, I still had achieved a major victory then. And, as with my other hill experience when I was hiking, I use that experience as a confidence booster when I am confronted with a new situation where I need to dig deep in order to accomplish something. Because my goal was specific, I can look back on it for inspiration, knowing that since I succeeded then, I can succeed in the future. If I had only had vague goals about "getting better" at running, or "improving," or "running harder," it would have been much harder to draw on them for inspiration because I wouldn't have clear evidence that I had really succeeded at something.

Also, since it is now relatively easy for me to get up that hill, doesn't that indicate that I am not working as hard? In a sense, it *does* indicate that. Since I am in better condition, I don't have to work as hard to get the same results. If I was working with a vague goal such as "I will work harder at my running," I could easily begin to feel like I was failing, when, in fact, it is only because I am improving that I don't have to work as hard. Or, I would only feel that I was being successful when I was accomplishing something on the order of getting up that hill, which is not something that I would be able to manufacture every day. You want to watch out for these traps because they are easy to fall into. With specific goals you can keep close tabs on your progress, but with vague goals, you can lose sight of what you are accomplishing and feel like you are failing when you are actually succeeding.

Step Five: Have a timeline for the accomplishment of your goal.

On first thought, nobody seems to like this one. I guess it's natural to be a little hesitant when it comes to doing something like this because it seems like we're putting undue pressure on ourselves. But this isn't the way we should approach the idea. For one thing, we ultimately work better, or at least a little harder, when there is some kind of deadline motivating us. I know that I have a tendency to drift a little when the completion of a project or task doesn't have a back end to it. I have also found that I can get a lot more out of myself, even in little things, when I give myself a timeline. For example, grading papers isn't my favorite activity, but it's something that I have to do. What I used to do was to complain to myself about it and put it off whenever possible. (Of course, this sounds just like the students' reaction to *doing* the assignments in the first place!) By learning to apply the same stuff that I am teaching you here, I changed my approach. Now, when I have to grade a stack of papers, I look at the clock and tell myself that these papers will be finished by whatever o'clock. I have to tell you that it makes a tremendous difference in the amount of work I get done.

For example, during my last summer school session, I got a stack of finals that would have taken well over an hour if I hadn't put any deadline on the task. I looked at the clock and saw that I had thirty-five minutes before the end of the class. The students were working on another section of the test, so without even thinking about it, I told myself that I'd finish grading the papers before the end of class. It didn't seem like enough time, given the normal pace at which I grade papers, but I attacked the pile and never let up, finishing with two or three minutes to spare.

There are a couple of important points to be learned from this seemingly insignificant incident. And, yes, I picked this example as an illustration because it *was* a little thing, the kind you can find any day of the week. I want you to realize that you don't need to find major, earthshaking events to put these principles into action. Being consistent in the little stuff, as any successful person will tell you, is far more important to your overall success than overlooking the details while you search for the gigantic challenges.

It is not your passing inspirations or brilliant ideas
so much as your everyday mental habits
that control your life.
--Paramahansa Yogananda

First, putting a timeline on my goal allowed me to reach down and come up with a level of effort that I didn't normally use when grading papers. This is significant because, like I said, I *don't* like grading papers. By knocking them out in such a short span, I realized again that whether or not I enjoyed doing the task had nothing to do with the level of energy I put into it. This is such a key point that I am tempted to say that it might be the most important thing you could learn at this point in your efforts. So let me say it again in big letters: WHETHER OR NOT YOU LIKE DOING SOMETHING SHOULD HAVE *NO* BEARING ON THE AMOUNT OF EFFORT YOU PUT INTO IT, IF IT IS IMPORTANT TO YOUR SUCCESS AND HELPS YOU ACHIEVE YOUR GOALS.

But you know what? Something interesting happened when I put the timeline on the goal. Instead of griping about having to grade the papers, my attention went to whether or not I could get them done in time. I was in the middle of a challenge and it became like a game. So, instead of having a bad time, I was having a lot of fun doing something I'd rather not have to do at all.

But, what if I hadn't gotten the papers done in time? After all, I just chose a time based on what was left of the period--I didn't stop to think whether I could do it or not. (Which is a good thing, because if I had, I probably wouldn't have gone through with it, limiting beliefs being what they are.)

> I am looking for . . . men who have an infinite capacity
> to **not** know what can't be done.
> --Henry Ford

Ultimately, it wouldn't have made much difference because the timeline wasn't the most important thing. Whether or not you achieve your goal within the timeline you set, you will work much harder and get more done than if you hadn't set one at all. Obviously, when you are working on goals that take more planning and consideration than ones like my paper grading goal, you don't want to just set any old timeline, thinking "hey, if I make it, ok, if I don't, fine." You want to sincerely work to get done under the wire. It's best to think about how long it would take you to do the task and then set a timeline which is shorter than you thought it would take. That way, you will be pushed to work a little harder than you would have ordinarily. Just make sure you understand that if you work hard and don't meet your timeline, you shouldn't feel like you failed; you just needed more time to accomplish your goal. (For example, I missed the first timeline for the completion of this book, so I made a new one and moved on. I missed that one too, but, finally, here it is, under the wire for the third one I set.) Timelines are important, but you needn't be tied to them to the point of beating yourself up about it. They are there to guide and motivate you, not punish you.

Step Six: Just because you don't initially know how you are going to accomplish a goal doesn't mean you shouldn't pursue it.

Even though I talked about writing out your goals and plans in detail, there's no reason for you to expect to have all of your plans figured out before you start. If you *do* have a clear idea of how to go about what you are after, fine. But, if having everything ready to go before you started was necessary, many successful people would not have been able to accomplish much of what they have. There have been many cases where the only thing that was clear at the beginning was the strong desire to achieve their particular goal. And, ultimately, that desire is the only thing that's necessary in order to get started. Remember this: *Your willingness to do it is by far the most important factor in your achieving your goal.* You see, there are many people who will not start anything until they have everything figured out. The sad thing is that they wind up never getting to that point, so they never take action. You don't want to be one of these people.

> He that leaveth nothing to chance
> will do few ill things,
> but he will do few things.
> --Earl of Halifax

If there is something that you really want to pursue but don't know how to go about it, don't let that stop you. Just start working towards it in any way that you can. What you will see happen is that as you begin pursuing your goal, invariably, ideas and assistance will become available to you. (One of the main reasons why this happens is discussed in detail in the next chapter, so I will hold off on it for now.) So, don't limit your goals to what you think *might* be possible or what you think you might be able to do. These limiting beliefs do not serve you well; they are *not* your friends. If you want something, go after it, regardless of whether or not you know exactly how you will get it. The desire to achieve something goes a long way towards opening doors you aren't even aware of when you get started.

> Whatever you can do, or dream you can--begin it.
> Boldness has genius, power, and magic in it.
> --Johann Wolfgang Goethe

What You *Become*
is More Important than What You Get

Of course, just setting goals will not in itself get the job done. After all, having a road map might tell you how to get where you are going, but it isn't going to drive your car for you! You are still going to have to do the work in order to make your goals become reality. But having the goals is a critical step in achieving your dreams.

So, now you have a better understanding of why goals are such an important element of your success. Before moving on, however, I want to raise an important point that sometimes gets lost in all of the emphasis on goals. If you have come this far, you are most likely serious about succeeding. And, because of this, you will be setting and achieving many goals, now and in the future. But, there is one point you must understand if you want to be truly successful: The *kind* of person you become because of your goals is more important than the goals themselves. You probably haven't heard the old saying that I just made up that says: "Success doesn't make you any happier; it just brings you better-dressed misery." In other words, there are many supposedly "successful" people living unfulfilled lives filled with frustration and despair. Does this mean that you can't be successful and happy at the same time? Of course not. It just means that it is important to think about what you are going after, why you are going after it, and what kind of person you will become in the process. For example, someone who uses this stuff to become a successful lawyer because that is what is expected of them, even though they never cared for being a lawyer, is not going to be successful, even if they wind up becoming the head partner of the biggest law firm in town. Why? Because they have followed someone else's dream, and not their own.

There are more elements to success than making a lot of money or having a prestigious career. Although there is nothing wrong with wanting these things, you need to give attention to other aspects of your life as well, aspects that many people seem to forget about when they think about success. For instance, would you want to be a rich and famous person who suffered from chronic ulcers and generally wretched health? How about a rich and famous person who went through one divorce after another, or who couldn't get along with his or her family and people in general and had no peace of mind whatsoever? No one would pick these types of situations if they had the choice. And, regardless of what some people will try and tell you, you *do* have a choice. Success doesn't mean making enemies and sacrificing other aspects of your life in order to achieve your goals.

You can, and should, strive for leading a balanced life which pays proper attention to your material, social, spiritual, and health concerns. And your goals, far from being ends in themselves, are most valuable when they serve as the means to aid you in acquiring this balanced life, which is far more fulfilling, and therefore, successful, than just getting stuff and being hated by everybody you clobbered on the way up the ladder. So pay attention to the types of goals you set because they will be what determines the direction you travel in. And, despite what many people would have you believe, the more you help other people, the more you yourself are helped. Honest.

Of course, once you determine your goals, you should program them into your mind daily by imaging what your life will be like and how you will feel when you have accomplished them. Get excited about them. After all, they *are* going to change your life.

Chapter Five

Focus--
Hey, Look at That!

Tell me what you pay attention to,
And I will tell you who you are.
--Otrega Y Gasset

Now is All You Get

Yes, you should be excited about your goals, since they do have the power to dramatically change the quality of your life. But you don't want your life to consist only of *possible* future successes because that is a sure way of missing out on the present, the only part of life that you actually get to walk around in.

So many people fail to truly live because they spend most of their time either worrying about the future or feeling guilty about the past. You definitely want to watch out for these twin traps of misery. Successful people, while mindful of the past and future, live in the present. As I said, what you become through accomplishing your goals is far more important than the goals themselves. In other words, the *process* is just as important as the results you get from it. If you want to find the truly sad people in the world, look no further than those who have ignored this fact. There they are, wondering what to do now after they have accomplished everything they set out to do, often after years of hard work, and they still don't feel fulfilled because they ignored the present while always looking to the future. What they didn't realize is that the future never gets here, so when they accomplished their goals they were left asking themselves "is this all there is?" And there they were, wondering why they felt so empty. Not a situation you want to be in.

So, if you aren't particularly interested in being miserable today while waiting for tomorrow's happiness (which never seems to get here), you will want to pay close attention to the next three chapters because they deal with the keys to getting the most out of *right now:* focus and state.

> Live each present moment completely
> and the future will take care of itself.
> --Paramahansa Yogananda

Simple Doesn't Mean Easy

Focus and state are not complicated concepts, which probably explains why people generally have the hardest time getting a handle on them. That concepts so simple can possibly have such a powerful effect on their lives is something many people cannot bring themselves to believe. They think that if it really were so simple, they would be doing it, and, since they aren't, it can't be that simple. Classic circular reasoning!

But these people are making the mistake of confusing "simple" and "easy." What's the difference? A couple examples should make it clear. Have you ever seen someone spin a basketball on their finger? It's quite simple. Here's how you do it: Hold your hand up with your fingers extending upwards and your palm facing away from your body. Place a basketball on your fingertips and twist your wrist really hard so that it now faces your body. This will cause the basketball to spin quickly. Immediately after spinning the ball, extend your index finger straight up, placing it underneath the basketball. Hold it there as the basketball spins. That's all there is to it. Now, let's try another simple task--a handstand. Bend over and place your hands flat on the ground about shoulder's width apart. Kick your feet up so that they are straight over your hands and keep them there, extending your arms and body fully. What could be simpler? But not so easy at first, huh? All of the concepts and techniques you are learning about in this book are simple, but they may not be easy to do at first. That's ok--it's why they invented practice. Don't fall into the trap of dismissing something because it seems too simple.

And, while we're at it, don't be one of the many "Well, sure, I could do it, but . . . " people, either. These folks are always around, and they are forever ready to stop you from excelling at anything because your success makes them look bad. As the old saying goes, people are like crabs in a tub--if one tries to climb out, the others will reach up and pull it back in! You are going to be climbing out of the tub of the ordinary; don't let other people pull you back in because they are jealous of your success.

You Can't Focus on Everything

Anyway, *focus* is simply what you are paying attention to at any given moment. It doesn't sound like a big deal, but the effect it has on your everyday life cannot be overstated. In fact, ultimately, *the quality of your daily life is directly determined by your focus.*

This one's going to take some explaining, so here we go. Of all of the things going on around you, what are you aware of right now as you read this? Maybe you are aware of the words on the page, but are you aware of the weight of the book in your hand? How about the temperature in the room? Is it too hot, too cold, just right? Is there any noise in the room--other people talking, clock buzzing, window rattling, heater or air-conditioner noise, refrigerator noise, traffic outside? What about the brightness or dimness of the light, the color of the walls, the texture of the rug or the surface of the floor, the shape of the tiles on the ceiling? Are there any smells you hadn't noticed? Food cooking in the kitchen, your perfume or cologne, your neighbor's lack of perfume or cologne? How does your back feel sitting in that hard chair? Are your legs stiff from running, or soccer practice yesterday? On and on it goes.

You see, your conscious mind doesn't pay attention to everything that is happening around you. It can't, since to do so would overwhelm you because there's too much happening at any one time. Now, if your conscious mind can't pay attention to all of the things going on *around* you, do you think it can pay attention to everything that is happening *within* you--your emotions, plans, fears, dreams, goals, regrets, likes, dislikes, hopes, etc.? Obviously, it cannot. You know from your own experience that in order to pay close attention to one thing, whether a feeling or an outward event, you have to stop paying attention to something else. What you are doing when you divert your attention in this way is shifting your *focus*.

You *Do* Choose Your Focus, So What Will You Choose?

Since there's too much going on around you, and within you, for you to deal with at one time, you have to choose, or focus on, a particular portion. So, how do you decide what you are going to focus on? Well, if you're like most people, you don't even think about it and just follow your habitual patterns of focus. Of course, if your habitual patterns are generally negative, your focus isn't serving you very well, is it?

For illustrative purposes, let's look at an average school day from the point of view of someone who has a negative focus. "First of all, as a general premise, school sucks. Period. After all, the teachers are the worst. They're basically bitchy, and they are only concerned with how they can ruin my day. I mean, what are they *doing* up there? They lecture me into a coma with a constant, never ending stream of useless information that has *nothing* to do with real life, right? Then, when they're done with that, they give me some impossible test, or stupid writing assignment that has nothing to do with anything I care about. And, if I were to bother writing about something that I *did* care about, they're only going to flunk me anyway. Why do I have to bother with this stuff? Science, math, history . . . what's it got to do with *my* life? And English?! Hey, I can already *speak* the language. Why do I have to keep learning about it?

"And, as if the teachers weren't bad enough, I have to put up with all of these nerds that insist on doing whatever they can to make me look bad--these goody-goodies with their raised hands and right answers and everything turned in on time. My God, do they have a life or what? And, please, don't even talk to me about PE, or the food in the cafeteria. Just wake me when this nightmare is over, and let me know when I can get *on* with my life!"

We are Trained to See a Negative Focus

I wish I could say that the above portrayal is an exaggeration, but, in my experience, it is all too common. Easy, too. With such an outlook, a student can blame everything on someone else, right? Of course, I can't blame a student too much for having such a focus. After all, in our society it's easy to adopt such an outlook because we are trained to focus on the negative, aren't we? Look at the evening news: "This is Dan Rather reporting from somewhere special with today's menu of fresh catastrophe. Our specials are: (and you may sing along.)

> Twelve wars a raging
> eleven generals lying
> ten crooks in congress
> nine brokers cheating
> eight treaties broken
> seven scandals brewing
> six spies a singing

                    five
                 failed
                      banks
              four forests cut
             three drug lords
              two oil spills
        and the recession isn't over!"

Look, people: Every day, thousands of planes take off without
a hitch, but if one crashes, it's film at eleven. A million teachers
and a million preachers are doing a world of good and the only
thing you're going to see on TV is some misfit child abuser or
con man or something equally pleasant.

Just Another Rotten Day Made to Order

Ok, just because a negative focus is easy to have, that doesn't
mean you want one. In fact, think about the price you pay for
having one. What if you were like the student with the negative
focus described above? What kind of experience would you be
likely to have on a daily basis? Each day, you get to school,
expecting everything about it to suck. And, of course, you are
right. It does suck! And, so, we come to the main point
concerning focus, the reason why it is essential to understand the
key role it plays in your life: Generally, *you get what you focus
on*. In other words, if you go looking for it, you're probably
going to find it. You want to see everything in shades of gray?
Fine, gray it is. You want every class to be boring? Boring they
will be. You need a reason why this assignment is stupid? No
problem; your brain will give you three or four reasons without
breaking a sweat. Are your classmates jerks? Well, hell, look at
them! That one acts like this, this one acts like that, and that
group over there is so pathetic that once again you are afraid
you're going to have to run out of the room screaming just to
keep from throwing a chair at them. Just like the commercials

say--you want it, you got it! If you focus on it, that's what you are
going to see.

> Be careful how you interpret the world:
> It *is* like that.

The Return of the "Reality" Demons

Now, is this negative focus your only option? Obviously, it isn't,
but the positive approach has generally come to be seen as one
that is "not being realistic." But, did you ever stop to notice
which people keep emphasizing the negative end of things? Try
this simple test. The next time someone begins feeding you this
negative line of "being realistic," take a look at their everyday
behavior and ask yourself this question: "If I could change the
way I am with just a snap of my fingers, would I want to be like
this person?" I'm willing to bet your answer would be "no."
Think about it. Have you ever heard this line of negativity coming
from any of the successful people that you know in your personal
life, or the ones you've read about or seen on TV? Again, I'm
willing to bet that you haven't, because another trait of successful
people in all fields is a positive focus.

But having a positive focus *doesn't* mean telling yourself that
everything is just exactly wonderful. "Jeez, I had it all wrong! All
of my classmates are great, all of my classes are greater, and all
of my teachers are the greatest. I wish we could do this school
thing twelve hours a day. And, if we must have weekends off,
couldn't we at least have twice as much homework?" Perhaps,
with a great deal of time and effort, you *could* convince your
brain that you really believed it, but there's a better way.

Stop Looking for What You Don't Want to Find

Remember, since you can't consciously take in everything going
on around you, or within you, you are always focusing on only
a portion of the picture. But, the great thing about this is that you

get to *choose* where your focus will be. So, if you don't want to see the worst in every situation, all you have to do is stop looking for it. That's the first and biggest step. And, of course, just like I mentioned during our discussion on stating goals, you don't want to begin by telling yourself, "I will not focus on the negative," because by doing so, you will still be looking at the negative, since you are focusing on what you don't want, instead of what you do want. Instead, ask yourself "what is positive about this situation?" If you are willing to persist beyond the first five seconds and the answer, "nothing," your brain will provide you with *real* answers and your focus will begin to shift.

A Positive Focus Isn't Pretending

Often, when the subject of shifting one's focus comes up, someone will ask whether it is wrong to pretend that things are different than they are. After all, if an assignment is stupid, it's stupid; if a teacher's boring, she's boring.

> There is nothing either good or bad
> but thinking makes it so.
> --William Shakespeare

When I discussed beliefs, I said that it didn't matter whether the belief was accurate or not. If you believed it, you behaved as if it were true, so for you, it *was* true. It's the same with focus. Whatever you choose to focus on becomes your reality because you are going to see the whole picture from that angle. It's not a question of whether your focus is right or not. Like the old saying about the glass being half full or half empty, the point isn't which one is the right answer since, obviously, both answers are equally correct. So don't worry about whether your focus is accurate. If it works, it works. And, again, don't let anybody else tell you that you aren't being realistic if you aren't looking for the worst in everything. That negative view isn't any more "realistic" than any other. Through working with the same material you are learning here, I have learned to shift my focus from negative to positive by looking for what's good about a situation instead of what's wrong with it. Instead of trying to continually resist everything that comes my way by saying it's boring or stupid, I ask myself how I can benefit from it. And when I see the dramatic improvement in the quality of my everyday life, how much happier I am on a consistent basis, I can only smile at those negative souls that keep trying to pull me down into the world of their "reality." I've been on both sides of the fence, and I know the grass is greener on *my* side! Anyone can make the same changes I did, if they're willing to practice and work towards being consistent. So it might as well be you, right?

The mind's direction is more important than its progress.
--Joseph Joubert

Link Your Focus to Your Goals

Admittedly, it's not that easy to change your focus just like that. If you've been working from a negative standpoint, you've had lots of time to program that pattern into your brain. It isn't going to change just because you wake up one day and say "no more negative focus!" You're going to need to keep on top of your thought patterns. Luckily, you now have extra tools to make your job easier. An excellent way to work with changing your focus is to tie it to other areas that you are working with, making a larger program that pushes your whole life in a more successful direction. Remember, the more energy you put into something, the more momentum you build up. The more momentum you build up, the more energy you get to work with. It's a great loop to get on.

So, instead of trying to change your focus all by itself, link your new focus to your new identity, beliefs, and goals. This makes your task easier, since all parts of your overall success program are working together, thus creating the ever desired momentum. (It also shows you up front whether or not your parts *are* working together.) For example, as I said before, most students don't do as well as they could because when it comes to determining if they are going to do an assignment, or how much effort they will put into it, they get caught up in whether or not they like the assignment or the subject or the teacher or whatever. If you have this problem, your focus is not being aimed in the right direction and isn't serving you well.

But, your focus can serve you much better if you link it to a goal. For example, say you had the following goal to drive your focus: "I will do all of my assignments immediately and to the best of my ability." Your positive focus and your goal can then work together to help you succeed. Instead of getting bogged down in whether you like the teacher or assignment, your focus is on your goal, so when you get an assignment, you jump on it right away. If you are committed to achieving your goal, *it* becomes the most important part of the equation, not how you feel about geometry or vocabulary or whatever. By making this simple (but, at first, not always easy) adjustment, you save an incredible amount of energy that you would normally use on resisting the assignment.

Focusing for Fun

Also, you have a lot more fun, because you are succeeding in an area where you used to have trouble. It becomes like a contest you have with yourself. You can go from "aaarrrgghh, I hate vocabulary; it's so booorrriinnggg. I'd rather poke sticks in my eye" to "Ok, let's see how fast I can get this finished and still make sure I learn all the words." With the old way, you had lots of misery while the idea of doing the vocab was in the back of your head when you were procrastinating--and you still had to do it anyway. When you finally did it, your heart wasn't in it, so you didn't do that well. And, you probably did poorly on the test because you weren't prepared. That's no fun beforehand, no fun during, and no fun afterwards. Not much of a chance to enjoy yourself, is there?

But, imagine having fun doing assignments you used to dread. It *can* happen, you know. When you get the assignment, you don't focus on the vocab, but on your goal. So, instead of trying to find a way out of doing it, you go right after it because that's what you *do*! (Can you see how identity comes into this?) Now, where there was once pain in getting an assignment, you now get pleasure because you are anticipating a chance to achieve your goal, and that feels good. While doing your vocab, you aren't doing it half-heartedly because you know your goal is to do your work to the best of your ability. Again, accomplishing your goal is where your focus is, and you get pleasure from doing well on the assignment. By doing well on the assignment, you are naturally prepared for the test, so you do well on that, too. Unlike before, you now have fun beforehand, fun during, and fun afterward. And, nowhere along the line did you have to talk yourself into liking vocabulary, because your success had nothing to do with liking vocabulary, per se. (Obviously, this applies not only to vocabulary, but to all subjects and assignments.)

RAS--Your Brain's Standard Equipment for Focus

There is another important aspect concerning focus and your goals which was touched on earlier. I said that, if you really wanted to pursue a goal, you should just focus on it and get started on it right away, even if you didn't know how you were going to accomplish it, because doors *will* open up for you, revealing needed information or resources to help you on your way. Now, this may sound like wishful thinking or magic, but it isn't.

Be bold--
and mighty forces will come to your aid.
--Basil King

As I said, at any instant, there is far too much happening within you and around you for your conscious mind to cope with. Therefore, your brain focuses on only a narrow portion of this incoming data. Since most people don't pay attention to their focus, they are at the mercy of the habitual patterns which have been established by years of uncontrolled focusing.

But the question to be asked is: why do we focus on what we do? The answer lies in a function of the brain known as the reticular activating system, or RAS. While this system is quite complex from a neurological standpoint, for our purposes it is quite simple. The RAS's function is to determine what we pay attention to or notice within the overwhelming flood of data we are continuously receiving. Here's how the RAS works. Let's say you just bought a new car, a Ford Mustang. What happens? Right after you get it, you begin seeing Mustangs all over the place. Mustangs in commercials, Mustangs in magazine advertisements, Mustangs on the road. Why? Is it because these cars just happened to appear everywhere all of a sudden? Obviously, that isn't the case. What is happening is that your purchasing a Mustang has made you focus on it, so you start seeing it everywhere. That's what your RAS does. It determines what data your conscious mind notices or pays attention to. After all, those Mustangs were there the whole time. But your focus wasn't. You could have passed ten of them on the way to school without noticing a single one. But, now that they are an important part of your life, you can spot one seven cars ahead as soon as you pull onto the freeway.

And so it goes with your goals. When you focus on a new goal, it becomes important to you and your RAS will alert you to anything connected to your goal that is going on within the flood of incoming data. Remember, *you get what you focus on*. Even if you don't know how it will happen, if you are serious and keep focusing on your goal, you *will* find information and resources to help you achieve it. It's what your RAS does, so use it.

Aim Your RAS Towards the Positive

But be careful. Remember when I discussed those people who only see the down side of everything? You now know that this is because their focus is trained to find the bad in any situation or idea. You also know now that the whole time they were focusing on the negative, there were many positive aspects to be seen right in front of them, but they didn't see them because their gaze was turned elsewhere (towards the negative.) This same principle applies to your goals. If you are focusing on reasons why something won't work, you *will* find them. But, if you focus on reasons why you will accomplish something, you will find *them*, instead. So, since you get what you focus on, focus on what you want to get, *not* on what you don't want.

Focus. It's a simple tool that can dramatically change the quality of your life. Use it properly and see the results it brings you.

See the good that lies so near.
Only learn to seize good fortune,
for good fortune's always here.
--Johann Wolfgang Goethe

Chapter Six

STATE: Part I
Posture

The greatest discovery of my generation
is that a human being can alter his life
by altering his attitudes of mind.
--William James
(Nineteenth century psychologist)

How are you feeling right now? Are you happy? Sad? Angry? Depressed, tired, excited, or bored? However you are feeling right now is the result of the state of mind you are in. This state of mind, which, from now on will be referred to as *state*, is the key to your ability, as well as your inability, to perform at the levels necessary to be successful. You may not have thought of this before, but even a casual examination of your own life will show you that it's true. Haven't you had times where you were unable to do something because of the mood you were in, or your energy level was so low, or you had an attitude? Haven't you also experienced times when, doing the same thing, you just cruised along, happy and energized, excited about what you were doing and knowing you would succeed without any problem? What was different? It wasn't your ability to accomplish the task that differed dramatically. It was your *state*. How many times have you heard someone say "it's all in your head"? Well, they're right! It *is* all in your head, because your behavior in any given situation is going to be influenced far more by your state than by anything happening on the outside.

Your State Determines How You Will React

There's a story that gives a classic illustration of how state affects our behavior. John was late for a meeting and was impatiently waiting for an elevator. When it finally arrived, it was packed. Instead of waiting for the next one, John decided to squeeze himself on, since he was behind schedule. As he was standing there, he felt a hard object, which he figured to be an umbrella handle, digging into his back. He didn't look to see who was jabbing him, but when they kept it up he could tell they were punishing him for forcing his way onto the full elevator. As the elevator was taking him to his floor, John began to get angry and started thinking about how rude people could be. The more he thought about it, the angrier he got. As he reached his floor, he was determined to give the jerk who was jabbing him a piece of his mind because people who were that inconsiderate deserved whatever they got. After everyone had filed off, he turned, expecting to see his tormentor. Instead, John saw an old blind woman and the cane which had been pressing against his back. Now, instead of anger, he immediately felt guilty for having had such thoughts about an old blind woman and quickly offered to help her off the elevator.

What was going on with John? In the space of a minute, he went from being outraged and wanting to tear someone's head off, to being overcome with guilt and rushing to give someone a hand. Nothing on the outside had changed in any way, but his *associations* about what was going on had changed. And it was his associations which determined his behavior, not the outside event.

It's Not the Thing, But Your Associations to It
that You React to

Think about it. It's not what happens to you on the outside that makes you behave in a certain way, because when something happens on the outside there isn't just an automatic process in your brain which decides how you are going to behave. As with John in the elevator, your *state* determines how you are going to respond. Even when it comes to your schoolwork! It's not the homework that you hate, and it's not the tests that you hate. If it were, how come some people hate these things while other people love them? The way you behave all depends on what you associate to the thing you are reacting to, what you are looking for from it. If you are looking for constant pain and sorrow, sure algebra will give it to you. But, if you are looking for a way to be successful at something, it will offer you that as well. *Your state is determined by what you associate to the things that happen to you, NOT the things themselves.* Like a test, for example. If you associate a bunch of negative baggage to it, it's the associations that you don't like, not the test. So, if you want to change the way you think about something, change the associations you link to it. Look at it and see the more positive things associated with it. Focus on the positive and your state will change towards the positive, focus on the negative and . . . well, you've already had enough of that, haven't you? Remember what I've been saying over and over--your brain just follows the directions that you give it.

To Consistently Succeed,
You Must Manage Your State

Most people just passively accept whatever state they are in, saying, "well that's just the way I feel right now." They have no idea that they can change their state. But it can be done, and *you* can do it. Understanding and a little practice are all you need.

Like I said in the last chapter, goals are important for our future success, but we don't want to forget about *right now* while we are planning for the future. Like focus, state is about right now. Your ability to effectively deal with your state right now does much to determine how well you do in the future because the road to the future is paved with a continuous series of right nows. A basic premise of this book is that everyone has within them great power and resources which will aid them in achieving whatever they are striving for. But most people fail to tap into these resources due to their limiting beliefs and the habitually negative states that they operate from. If you are spending most of your time right now in unresourceful states, you're not going to be getting the best out of yourself in the future. If you want to consistently succeed, you've got learn to take control, or *manage* your state.

Since your state is determined by the way your mind and body respond to the stimuli of your environment, I am going to divide our investigation of managing your state into the categories of mind and body, starting with the body, since it plays such a key part in state and, yet, most people are unfamiliar with its role.

Posture, or the Way You Use Your Body, is a Key to Your State

If there were three people in a room--one angry, one depressed, and one enthusiastic and happy--do you think you could tell which was which, even if they weren't saying anything? Of course, you could. After all, can't you tell when someone is upset without them telling you? How about when they are depressed? Haven't you asked a friend what was up, even though they insisted nothing was wrong? Well, what is it that clues you in to what they are feeling? You probably haven't thought about it before, but it's the way they are using their body. People that are depressed position their body in a certain way that lets you know that that's how they are feeling. You know how it is--they hang their head and look at the floor, they droop their shoulders and sigh, right? But what about someone who is happy and enthusiastic? Have you ever seen them use their body as if they were depressed? Well, if not, why not? Why is it that you can generally tell whether someone is happy or depressed, angry or whatever?

One of the major factors determining state is your *posture*, or the way you use, or position your body. I've said before that sometimes things are so simple that people don't want to believe that they work. This is especially true when it comes to posture. Our posture plays a profound part in determining how we feel, but many people refuse to even experiment with it. After observing people with this in mind, I've become convinced that most people are content to feel rotten because there are substantial benefits to be gained from feeling that way. I'm also convinced because I was an expert in the area of feeling rotten for more years than I care to admit.

Primary and Secondary Gain

I know it sounds crazy to say that someone would want to feel rotten by choice, but it's true. To make sense of this phenomenon, we have to consider *primary* and *secondary* gain. If you were taking a test in math, or writing an essay, or working on a science project, it seems reasonable to assume that you would want to get a good grade on it, doesn't it? Doing well on an assignment is the primary gain, and it's easy to understand because it's pretty obvious. It's the up front, logical answer to the question, "What's in it for me?" But secondary gain isn't that obvious, and most of the time, people don't consciously realize when they're pursuing it. For example, concerning general physical well-being, it seems logical to assume that everyone would want to feel as good as they could, right? Well, let's take a little quiz.

Most people would prefer a state where:
   a) they were filled with energy and enthusiasm.
   b) they had no energy and felt like they could barely get
      through the day.
Of course, the obvious answer is a. But the correct answer is b.
It's easy to see the primary gain of choice a: having abundant
energy is an invaluable aid, since, rarely being tired or depressed
or stressed out, you can do what needs to be done quickly,
efficiently, and enthusiastically. Well, who wants that!?

If you take a look around you, it doesn't take long to notice that
not too many people do. But, why not? This is where secondary
gain begins to make sense. When you have abundant energy and
enthusiasm, you don't have any *excuses* for not getting the job
done. Imagine that! I think if there's one thing that the average
person seems to love above life itself, it's a good excuse for
taking the responsibility for succeeding off of his or her
shoulders. Think about it. Whenever somebody can't get the job
done, whether it's homework, a good test score, a project, or
whatever, they look for an excuse. We've all done it at one time
or another, but what does it get us? We still fail, but with an
excuse, we feel *justified*. "Well, sure, I could have easily done it,
but . . . " And, of course, some excuses are better than others. If
your excuse is that you didn't study, or didn't pay attention, or
were out with your friends, nobody is going to have much
sympathy for your not getting the job done. And you know deep
down that you didn't put in the necessary effort. But, if you're
tired, or don't feel good, or are stressed out, there's more of a
chance that you will be excused to some degree, even if it's only
yourself who's doing the excusing. So, if not feeling well or being
tired all the time brings you the excuse you need to get you off
the hook for not performing successfully, then that is the
secondary gain of feeling rotten.

Your Posture Doesn't Follow Your State; It Does Much to Help *Create* It

Remember, in any given situation, our actions are based on our desire to gain pleasure and avoid pain. If feeling rotten helps you get out of doing something that you thought you were going to have trouble with, and there is more pleasure in avoiding the task than in doing it, then you will gladly feel rotten in order to avoid the pain of having to do the task. But, what if you are interested in succeeding and don't want to feel tired or stressed out because you find it getting in the way of your accomplishing your goals?

When we are tired,
we are attacked by ideas we conquered long ago.
--Friedrich Nietzsche

After a while, feeling rotten begins to bring more pain than the (secondary) benefits it brings. What if you are sick and tired of feeling sick and tired? Changing your posture, or the *way you use your body*, is a wonderfully effective way to change your state.

We don't usually think of the part that our bodies play in the way that we feel, but we should. Say somebody was depressed. Do you think that the way they position their body has anything to do with the way they are feeling? Most people, when considering the connection between state and posture, just assume that a person's state or attitude is a product of the mind, and that their posture just reflects that state. In other words, if I appear depressed (i.e., slumped shoulders, sighing, looking at the floor, etc.) it is because I *am* depressed; my posture is only mirroring my state. But, is it possible that using your body in a depressed manner can cause you to slip into a depression or deepen an already existing depression? Can you use your body in a way that makes you feel tired? Yes you can, and yes you do. You see, your posture doesn't merely *react* to your state and follow along passively; it plays an active part.

Using Your Posture to Feel Energized

Our brain and our body work together to determine how we feel. If you habitually adopt a posture of depression, or tiredness, your brain will act upon the signals it receives from your body and respond accordingly. As I've been saying all along, your brain is like a computer, in that it runs the program that you load into it. If, by your posture, you load a program which tells your brain that you feel tired, then your brain will accept the information and provide you with reasons to be tired, thereby *making you feel tired.*

But, what if you load in a program that has you feeling filled with energy? Since your posture helps determine your state, you can use this knowledge to your advantage. Let's assume that you are feeling tired, but don't really want to. (I emphasize not wanting to because I've already discussed secondary gain and the benefits that a person can get from feeling rotten.) What can you do to feel better? Well, the easiest way to feel more energetic is to adopt a posture of energy and enthusiasm. That's right, just act *as if* you were filled with energy. Move your body *as if* you were totally pumped with energy. Breath deeply like you do when you are filled with energy. *Be* like you would be if you were filled with energy and enthusiasm. Do you know what will happen if you do this with sincerity? You will *definitely* receive more energy and feel better. Just like that. I know it sounds too easy, but it *is* true.

> If you want a quality,
> act as if you already had it.
> --William James

Your Brain Acts on the Signals You Send It

If you think about it, it's not hard to understand how this concept of using your posture to switch gears on your state works. Why is it that you can recognize which person in the room is depressed or tired, and which one is energized and enthused? Isn't it because people generally use similar postures for similar states? You know when someone is angry because they *act* angry. You know when someone is tired because they *look* tired. You know when someone is enthusiastic because they *move* like they are enthusiastic. Well, if the way others look, act, and move allows you to recognize their states, doesn't it make sense that you can recognize the state you are in by the way you look, act, and move? It sounds funny, but this is what your brain does when it receives the various signals from your body. If your body is sending signals which the brain recognizes as those which are present when you are normally enthusiastic and energetic, it will interpret them to mean that you *are* enthusiastic and energetic and respond accordingly--even if only moments ago you were sending signals which said you were tired.

No Time for Being Tired

Now, you might say that this is only pretending to be energetic when you're really tired. But my question is this: Which state is real and which one isn't? I've said that up until I learned to use this stuff, I had been quite an expert in the fine art of feeling rotten. I accomplished this unfortunate skill by habitually loading programs of tiredness into my brain. Therefore, I was generally in a tired state, and it seemed pretty *real* to me.

One of the reasons it seemed so real was that I was going to college full-time while working forty hours a week as a caretaker for three mentally retarded adults at the house where they lived. Along with my regular eight-hour days, I worked alternate weekends which consisted of two fifteen-hour shifts, so my co-worker and I took it easy on those preceding Fridays, generally skipping the numerous learning and physical therapy programs that we were supposed to do every day and doing as little as we could possibly get away with. Once, on a Friday during finals, I had a grueling day at school and was absolutely wiped out by the time it was over. Since I was so exhausted, the only thought on my mind as I was driving to work was to get my co-worker to cover for me while I took a long nap. Our shift began fifteen minutes before our clients got home from their day program, and I usually got there about five or ten minutes before my co-worker did, so I was relaxing on the sofa when there was a knock at the door. Figuring it was him, I answered it and there was my supervisor, smilingly informing me that she was filling in for my co-worker that evening!

Now, my supervisor was of the drill sergeant variety, and she expected everything to be done properly, with enthusiasm, and no cutting any corners. On top of that, we didn't get along all that well, so she wasn't going to have much sympathy for my rough day. Instead of taking a nap and kicking back, I was going to have to do every program and no sitting down on the job. So, not having any say in the matter, that's what I had to do, and that's what I did. Well, a funny thing happened. After about three hours of nonstop running around, working with the clients, I noticed something. I wasn't tired at all. In fact, I was filled with energy for the remainder of the shift.

Which State Was the "Real" State?
At the time, I didn't know how this rapid state-shifting from exhausted to energized could happen, but now I do. After my rough day, I loaded my "feeling rotten" program into my brain's computer. But, when my supervisor showed up, I was forced to load my "energy and enthusiasm" program, instead. So, there I was, filled with energy because that was the posture I had adopted, and my brain reacted to the signals it was being sent. Now, which state was the "real" one, the exhaustion I felt when I arrived, or the energetic one I was forced to adopt because of the circumstances? After all, I *really* felt tired at the beginning of the shift, and I *really* felt energized the whole time I was running around and working with the clients.

Of course, by now, I am sure you know the answer: *It doesn't matter which state is "real" because your brain acts on the data it receives, regardless of whether it is "real" or not.* Your reality is shaped by your beliefs. If you believe that you are tired, you will feel tired. If you get caught up in the moment and "forget" to feel tired, you won't be tired.

Twenty Dollars Says You're Not *Really* Tired

It really *is* that simple, but students often have trouble believing that this is the case. One day, in the middle of a discussion about this concept, I asked the people who were tired to raise their hands, and more than half the class did so. I asked these students if they were really tired, or just a little tired, and they all said that they were really tired. They must have been, too, because all of them were displaying various postures of tiredness, whether slumped over, or leaning back, or just sitting there like lumps. Pulling a twenty-dollar bill out of my wallet, I told them that it was unfortunate that they were so tired because I was thirsty and, since the soda machine down the hall was empty, I was willing to offer the change to whoever could get me a soda from the cafeteria (which was way over on the other side of the school) and be back within two minutes. Without exception, each of the "really tired" students jumped up and insisted that they could do it, and that I should pick them! Putting the money back in my wallet, I told them that I just wanted to see how tired they really were, since, seeing that they were ready willing and able to run across the school and back, it looked to me like they were filled with energy. When they realized that I wasn't going to give the money away, they grumbled and went right back to the "tired" posture that they had started with. And you can be sure they were just as "tired" then as they were "energized" a few seconds before, when they thought they were going to get the money.

Move *as if* You Have Energy, and You *Will* Have Energy

Now that you have a better understanding of the effect that posture has on your state, how can you use it to your advantage in your daily life? I've already discussed how to get into a state of energy and enthusiasm--you just do it by using your body *as if* you were already in that state. Do this enough and you will develop a habit of being in this state, and then you won't have to worry about the *as if* anymore because it will turn into an *I am*!

In the meantime, what you want to do is learn ways in which to consciously use your body to reflect states of energy, enthusiasm, and success. To do this, think of times when you were in these states. Or, if you have trouble remembering personal experiences of these states, look at others who you know to be enthusiastic and successful. How do they walk? How do they stand? How do they sit? In short, how do they carry themselves?

What I'm talking about here is *not* cockiness; nobody is impressed with bragging and swaggering behavior. Instead, you want to move with assurance. Look at the successful person's walk. Isn't it true that successful people seem to walk as if they've got somewhere to be, as if they always have a purpose? It's a deliberateness instead of an aimlessness, and there is power in their stride. (But, please remember, it's not a strut; people who strut are generally regarded as having false pride. No one takes them seriously.) What you want to do is walk with power, with authority. Again, it's not an in-your-face kind of attitude, but one that is dignified, one that is respected and respectful. (As a student, you might have trouble believing that adults, especially teacher-type adults, are going to respect you. But you shouldn't worry about this. I can tell you without hesitation that teachers are always on the lookout for those students that are a cut above the rest, the ones that appear destined to be leaders. In truth, many times it's these students that get us through the day.)

As it is with walking, so it is with sitting and standing. You want to carry yourself with deliberateness, with authority. Sit up straight and stand up straight. It *does* make a difference. When you are consistently slouched over and looking as if you are about to fall asleep, you send messages to your brain and to other people's brains that you aren't operating at full speed. Is this the way you want to be perceived? If not, stand tall. After all, think of any of the heroes or people you really respect, whether in real life, in movies, on TV, or in books. Why do they all *look* like that? Why do they carry themselves that way, and why do we all react to them in the way that we do? It's because their posture is the posture that we have come to accept as that of those who are successful.

Therefore, if we adopt the same type of posture, we send our brains the same types of messages that our heroes send theirs, and we get the same results in the way of successful states from which to work. And, if we are operating out of successful states, the chances of our being successful improve dramatically.

Practice Your Posture of Success

So practice with your posture. It's easy, and you can do it at any time. The next time you are walking to class, think of how you would be walking if you had just aced the hardest test you had ever taken, or had just been named most valuable player in your school's division, or had just won an award for best whatever it is you would want to win, and *walk* that way. As soon as you do, you will feel a surge of confidence and energy. And remember, it *isn't* fake. You feel it is because you are sending signals of confidence and energy to your brain. And your brain is responding by sending back the same feelings that those who are already successful feel, which is why *they* carry themselves the way they do.

And, just as you do with walking, practice with sitting and standing. Think of how you would be doing either if you were feeling totally enthusiastic and successful and then do it. Take advantage of the loop that is created between body and mind: The more you use your body to create a positive state, the more positive your state will be, and the more positive your state, the more you will use your body to maintain that state.

I cannot overemphasize the importance of learning to make this shifting of posture a habit. Being tired or not feeling well are two of the most prevalent excuses I hear from students when they aren't doing as well as they know they could be doing, and they are excuses that are so easy to overcome. Please give this simple concept a fair try because you can get *so* much benefit from it. With a little practice, you can lay an excellent foundation for accomplishing everything else you want to do.

Chapter Seven

State: Part II
Self-Talk, Reframing,
and Gratitude

While posture plays a major part in state, it is only half of the story. Obviously, our mind plays a critical part in determining how we feel, and it does it in two major ways. Much of our state comes from what we *say to ourselves* and how we represent, or *picture things* in our mind.

If I had to think of the one thing that I probably do more than anything else every day, it would be telling people to stop talking. And, every now and then, they actually do stop--at least out loud, that is. But, inside their heads it's different, isn't it? You know what I'm talking about--that ever-present dialogue that we are having with ourselves. All day long it goes on, and all night, too. Let's face it, it never shuts up. One of the names for this internal dialogue is *"self-talk,"* and it plays a major part in your state.

While much of the time we are merely babbling to ourselves about things that don't have much bearing on our lives either way, a good portion of what we say *does* make a difference. In general, different people are talking about different things, and one of the things that separates those who are successful from those who aren't is the quality and the basic direction of their internal conversations.

We Use Self-Talk to Construct Our Reality

Self-talk is important because we *do* listen to it and use it to make sense of the world. Often, our conclusions about the way things are come from decisions we make during these conversations with ourselves. And, as we have seen from the example of John in the elevator, these conclusions *aren't* based on what's actually happening on the outside, but on our representations or interpretations of what's going on. In other words, we don't deal with reality itself, but with *our version* of reality. And an awful lot of our version of reality is derived from what we literally talk ourselves into. This is why it's so easy to have two people with wildly different interpretations of the same event.

As with anything else, we fall into habitual patterns with our self-talk and don't always think about, or pay conscious attention to what we are saying to ourselves. Using our analogy of the brain being like a computer, think of these patterns as being computer programs. (Yes, this is similar to what I said about beliefs being like software. Self-talk is a major component in the development of beliefs, and it works the same way in the brain.) When you load the program into the computer, the computer performs the functions without question. Likewise, your brain just follows the directions it is given. It doesn't stop and say, "Hey, this isn't right. This isn't true." It acts on the information coming from the conversations you are constantly having with yourself.

Most People's Self-Talk is Generally Negative

These habitual self-talk patterns can be hazardous if they are made up of negative messages. And, the sad part is that most people are often caught up in negative conversations with themselves. "I'm really not that smart." "I'm stupid." "I'm stupid looking." "I'm not good enough." "I'm just not any good at English/history/science/writing/spelling/math/studying/ sports/etc." "I suck at tests." "I always do everything wrong." "I can't work under pressure." "I'm an idiot.' "I'm tired.' "I don't feel good." "Things just don't work out for me." "This stuff may work for other people, but it isn't going to work for me." "I'll never get ahead." "I'm lazy." "I'll never get good grades." And the worst one of all, the one that gives us unquestioned permission to hang on to all of the other garbage, "That's just the way I am." On and on this stuff goes and our brains just take it in and produce the proper responses in our behavior. Whether these thoughts are actually true or not makes absolutely no difference whatsoever. If you believe that that's the way it is, then *that's the way it is*.

Negative Self-Talk Undermines Your Efforts to Improve

So, what are the consistent messages that *you* are hearing? What programs are you playing day after day, week after week, year after year? These programs that you continually play determine the direction you will be moving in. If the programs you load into your brain through your self-talk are negative, you can see what harm they are doing to you in your inability to achieve the results that you really want. After all, how can you be expected to get any positive work done over an extended period if you are constantly bombarding yourself with this junk?

If you want to move in a positive direction, you had better start *consciously* playing some positive programs. It's not a matter of just thinking positively; this stuff is programmed *far* deeper than conscious thought. It's in your subconscious and you react to it automatically. You know how it is. After every report card, you make a resolve to do better *this* quarter, to do all of your homework, to study, to do everything as soon as you get the assignment, and to not mess around in class. And it works for a couple of hours, or days, or even a week or two. But then you fall into your same old patterns and start your same old habits all over again. And why? Self-talk. Underneath all of your wonderful effort to improve, you are still running the same negative programs through your internal dialogue. And the negative programs are going to win every time because they are more deeply ingrained.

Self-Talk Won't Just Shut Up

To turn things around, you just can't stop the programs. Your brain thrives on this self-talk, and if you want to experience sheer frustration, just try to get your self-talk to shut up. It's not going to! So, stopping your self-talk isn't the answer because *some* program *will* be played. The key to changing your negative self-talk programs is just that--change them! What you want to do is to *replace* the old, negative program with a more consciously directed positive program. Again, it's just like beliefs: If you are running a program that says "I'm lazy and can't get my work done," you need to *consciously* and *consistently* replace it with the opposite program that you would rather have: "I'm a hard worker who gets my work done." If you are running a program that keeps telling you that you can't do well on tests, turn it around and begin running one that tells your brain that you *do* do well on tests because you are prepared and confident.

You are What You are,
But Who Says You Have to Stay that Way?

Of course, if I suggest doing something like changing your self-talk programs, there is a part of you that is going to say, "Hey, I can't do that; it's a lie. I really *am* lazy" Well, sure you are, *if* that's the program that you consistently run. But, were you born lazy? Were you born stupid? Were you born a procrastinator? You don't even have to answer these questions because they're as ridiculous as they sound. Let's face it: you've talked yourself into your present state over a long period of time and found reasons to reinforce your beliefs. (Remember RAS, the function of the brain which decides what you will focus on? If not, go back and check out the end of the chapter on focus.)

But, talking yourself *into* your state is all you've done. You can talk yourself *out of it*, too. You just have to be willing to work at it. There's no rule that says you have to stay the way you believe yourself to be right now. If you *want* to change, you *can* change. (And, obviously, you want to change because if you didn't, you wouldn't still be reading this book.) Remember, the reality of the situation is what *you* make it. If you change your state, *reality* has a way of changing right along with it.

Taking Control of Something You Already Do Every Day

Also, if the idea of working with your self-talk programs seems strange, or if you're not sure that you can do it, don't worry. As with *all* of the techniques in this book, *you are already doing it!* You are not learning how to do anything new here. You are just taking conscious control of something you've been doing all of your life. It's not the skill that's new here, but the idea that you are doing it *deliberately* instead of having it just happen to you. And, of course, if you don't do it intentionally, you will still be doing it anyway; you just won't be doing it consciously, and you will not be in control of your state. It's kind of like being on a boat out at sea. If the wind is blowing and you have your sail up, you have control over the direction in which you travel. If you take down your sail, you don't affect the wind, you just lose control over the direction you will move in because you are at the mercy of the wind, which is going to blow whether your sail is up or not. Self-talk is like the wind: it's going to go on whether you are paying attention to it or not. The only question is whether or not you are going to do anything to control the direction in which it is going to move you.

> Take charge of your thoughts.
> You can do what you will with them.
> --Plato

Guidelines for Changing Your Old Self-Talk Programs

Ok, so how do you change your programs? We've already mentioned the key ingredients, but let's set them out in order.

Step One: Find the negative programs that you want to replace.

If you can spot your negative programs easily, fine. Sometimes, however, it's not easy to get a handle on the them because they often work in the subconscious mind. Don't worry too much about it if you can't come up with them right away. They'll either show up as you begin your work, or they will be overruled by your new programs if you program the new ones effectively. The important thing for you to do is to determine the areas that you want to concentrate on in order for you to more successfully achieve the goals you are pursuing. So look at your goals and see if you can spot any self-talk patterns that are holding you back. A good way to spot a negative programs is to take your goal and ask yourself, "Why can't I accomplish this immediately?" After you've asked the question, listen to the response you get from your brain. If there are negative programs connected with this area, they will probably make themselves known as objections or fears or reservations.

Step Two: Find the positive programs you want to use as replacements.

Look at the negative programs you discovered when examining your goals and consider what the opposite programs would be. Be sure to frame them in language that is *positive* and that concentrates on what you want to accomplish, instead of what you want to avoid. For example, if you are designing a program to overcome your feelings of inadequacy when it comes to getting assignments done, you would want a program that says something like "I have the skill and the discipline needed to get my assignments done on time." And, as I've said when discussing identity, beliefs, and imaging, don't worry if you don't feel that you've been behaving in this way up to this point. Your previous self-talk has put limits on your behavior, and these changes in your self-talk will reinforce your new belief. As you continue to work, you will see a positive loop form: positive self-talk creates positive results, and positive results create more positive self-talk. Together, these elements create a new belief that reinforces your new positive identity, which further strengthens the whole process. Yes, this stuff all works together and you can now begin achieving the kinds of results that you've only dreamed about!

Step Three: Be consistent in your practice.

Like everything else, the more you practice your positive self-talk, the better you are going to get. Remember what you are doing here. You are working towards replacing negative programs that may have been running for years. This replacement isn't going to happen with just one or two attempts. You've got to keep at it. It *is* going to take some time, but, fortunately, you will be working *deliberately*, and you will be doing this work in conjunction with other techniques. This concentration of effort and techniques will make things happen in a much faster time-frame than the haphazard way that you initially did these things when you weren't consciously paying attention to what you were doing. So, be consistent and diligent in your practice. It *isn't* hard, and it *doesn't* take a lot of time. It only takes regularity. The few minutes you spend each day doing this stuff will pay off a thousand times over and will continue to bring you rewards long after you are out of school because these techniques can be applied to whatever area of your life you want to improve.

Step Four: Find a regular time to practice.

First thing in the morning and before you go to bed are both excellent times to work at this, but you can do it anytime that is comfortable for you. Just make sure that you are as consistent as possible because we are creatures of habit. (Ok, so we are mostly creatures of *bad* habits, but we're out to change that, aren't we?) The more consistent you are with practicing at regular times, the easier it is to establish the habit of practice. This habit is something you definitely want to install because it is easy to get swept away in the everyday events that constantly grab your attention. And you know how easy it is to get lost in stuff and forget to do something. Also, without a clearly established practice routine, it is easy to get caught up in the "Oh, I'll do it tomorrow" rut. Many days, weeks and months can slip by this way, and soon you can find yourself in the same place that you were *last* year: almost just about ready to finally begin to get started on commencing to get this stuff together!

So work hard to set up a regular routine. Then, if you want to do some extra work with the techniques when you have a spare minute or two, fine. Any additional practice strengthens your gains, but without the regular routine, you will find it difficult being consistent.

Homeostasis

There is another good reason why you should work to establish a regular routine. Unfortunately, it's the same reason why you might find it hard to do so at first. There is a concept called *homeostasis*, and it plays an important part in our lives. Homeostasis is the tendency of a system to maintain internal stability by resisting changes or disruptions, and it's one reason why it is sometimes hard to make lasting changes in your routine. Homeostasis is usually discussed in relation to biology because it is an important element in keeping the different bodily systems functioning properly. An example of homeostasis would be the body's immune system fighting off a disease or healing a cut. But homeostasis applies to systems of all kinds, whether they are institutions, governments or *your* usual routine.

We all have regular routines that we fall into, and homeostasis works to keep those routines going. This is why, for example, it is hard at first for people to lose weight, or to keep it off once they do. When any change is introduced into the system, in this case the system being your behavior, there is a degree of resistance to it. So, your initial efforts to alter your behavior will be met with resistance, due to homeostasis. But, if you keep at it with regularity, the same homeostasis will begin to help you maintain your new routine. For this to happen, however, you will have to be consistent in your efforts. If you only do it sporadically, your chances of actually maintaining the changes you want will not be good because of homeostasis. Therefore, if homeostasis can either be your enemy or your ally, why not choose to make it your ally? Instead of continuing to play the negative programs and wondering why you aren't getting anywhere, be consistent with the programming of your positive self-talk and you will find yourself working from a positive, resourceful state with greater frequency than you thought was possible.

If You Don't Like Reality, Reframe It

Posture and self-talk play a large part in determining your state, but another important element in creating state is the way you represent, or picture things to yourself. Remember, we don't really experience the reality of any given situation; we *interpret* the situation based on the filters comprised of our beliefs and state. As I said in the beginning of the last chapter, *your state is determined by what you associate to the things that happen to you, not by the things themselves.* These associations make up the frame through which we see the picture of the event. If we change the frame, we can change the way we feel about things. This is what happened to John in the elevator: Initially, he was quite angry because he thought someone was deliberately being rude to him. But when he saw the old woman, he changed his associations from ones of anger at someone being mean to ones of compassion for an old woman. This process of changing associations is called *reframing* because the frame is the *meaning* which we associate to the event. If we shift the frame, we shift the meaning, and, ultimately, our state.

Do Some Situations Have a Definite Meaning? Maybe

Some people might say that certain situations have obvious meaning and that there are definite responses that one should have in reaction to them. They would say that in the elevator story, John obviously and certainly would have helped the old woman. Maybe. But there is an ancient story from China which deals with the "obvious" and "certain" meaning of events.

There was an old farmer who lived in a poor village. He was better off than most of the villagers, since he had a fine horse which he used on his farm. One day, his horse ran away and the other villagers lamented about how unfortunate this was. The farmer replied, "Maybe."

After a few days, the horse came back to the farm and along with it were two wild horses. This time, the villagers were excited at the farmer's good fortune, but all he said was, "Maybe."

Excited about the new additions to the farm, the farmer's son tried to ride one of the wild horses. He was thrown from the horse and broke his leg. The villagers were quick to offer their condolences, since this meant that the son could not help his father work the farm. The farmer only replied, "Maybe."

A few days later, officers from the military came to the village looking for young men to draft into the army. Because the farmer's son had a broken leg, he wasn't drafted. When the villagers told the farmer how lucky he was, he only replied, "Maybe."

Reframing Allows You to Tap Greater Resources

Not many of us have this simple farmer's ability to look at events so calmly. In a similar situation, most of us would regard a broken leg or a lost horse as bad news, or two new horses or not being drafted as good news. But this doesn't mean that these events automatically come with these obvious meanings, as the farmer was wise enough to see. Usually, when something happens to us we rush to *assign* a meaning to the event and then base our reactions on the meaning we have assigned. But we *are* only reacting to our interpretation.

There's a story in the business world about a guy who made a mistake on a business deal which resulted in his company losing a nine million-dollar contract. He was called into the company president's office, and, before the president could say anything, he blurted out, "Look, I know you have to fire me, but . . . " The president's eyes widened and he said, "Fire you? I can't fire you. I've just spent nine million dollars training you!" Now, that's reframing!

Learning to Reframe Mistakes

This idea of reframing is critical when you've made a mistake. Normally, when we look back on mistakes, we get upset or maybe feel embarrassed. But, in general, don't we learn more from our mistakes than we do from the good stuff that we do? After all, when things are going along smoothly, we tend to cruise along with them; but when we screw up, we pay more attention because we have to think about what we did wrong and how to fix it or make sure we don't have to go through it again the next time. Since the *meaning* of an incident is entirely up to you, you can either emphasize the fact that you made a mistake and feel stupid or whatever, or you can reframe and emphasize the value that came from your learning something useful. This reframing of mistakes is something that successful people do, and you, too, can learn to turn something that seemed negative into something positive if you work with managing your state.

Of course, as I've said, this doesn't mean just pretending that everything is wonderful, because, let's face it, sometimes things don't seem too wonderful. But, some of the most significant victories you will ever have will come in the face of great difficulty. It's not in saying that everything is wonderful that reframing has its value, but in the ability to look at a situation or circumstance and *see what can be gained from it* to help you succeed in your goals.

Adversity introduces a man to himself.

A great little trick that is related to mistakes and your state is learning to shift out of "idiot mode" and back into a state which is more productive. When you screw something up and start feeling like an idiot, stop for a few seconds and go and do something else that you know you can do well. It doesn't have to be a big thing, or anything involved. You only need a few seconds. Just make it something you are good at. In fact, you don't even need to actually do it; you can *image* it for a few seconds. This is an effective way of regrouping, of shifting your state away from the "Oh, I'm such an idiot" mode and putting it back in the "See, I can do this" state. Then you can return to what you were doing with a better state of mind and get better results.

So what you want to do is practice working with your state and adding ways to positively shift it, just like you learned to do with your focus (by tying it to your goals, for example) because, as you have surely seen by now, all of these tools work together and are made up of a lot of the same elements.

Ask and You Shall Receive

There is an effective way to change your state that is so simple that most people won't even investigate it because they will think it couldn't possibly be that easy. But it is, if you practice. Remember, all of the stuff you are learning here is simple stuff, taken by itself. But when you start applying these techniques to your life, the results can be amazing. It just takes practice and the ability to try again when you screw up at first. It all happens in little steps, the smallest of which brings *big* results when followed by another small step. And don't worry if you mess up, or forget to do something, or fall back into an old pattern. Just get back to business and keep going.

> Fall seven times, stand up eight.
> --Japanese Proverb

So, if you want to change your state, there is a simple way to do it: just ask. That's right, just ask your brain and it will show you how. When you get in a situation that you normally don't care for, like an English or math class or something, just pose the question: "How can I have a better focus here, how can I improve my state?" If you really want to do it, and aren't just asking half-heartedly, your brain will show you an angle that you hadn't considered before. Remember, lot's of people, even though they are miserable most of the time, are happy to stay like they are. After all, there is a tremendous benefit to being able to blame everything on somebody or something else: They don't have to take responsibility for themselves.

But if you truly want to change your focus, your brain will be happy to help you, if you only ask it how. If you think this sounds funny, stop for a minute and realize all of the times your brain happily supplied you with reasons why you should have been in a rotten state, and how ready and willing you were to go right along with the reasons you received. Should it be so hard to get reasons why you should have a positive state? It isn't. Get into the habit of asking questions that lead your brain to come up with these reasons, and do it on a daily basis. The more you do it, the easier it becomes and the stronger your habit of accessing positive states becomes.

One trick I learned that improved my focus remarkably was to make a list of qualities that would improve the standard of my life, the qualities that I admired in people that I respected. Then, I framed the question, "How can I be more _____?" (Some of the qualities on my list are: considerate, determined, diligent, driven, efficient, enthusiastic, persevering, positive, etc.) By filling in the blank with the appropriate qualities on my list and *sincerely* asking the question, I started to receive quality answers that I could apply to the situation at hand. This is also an excellent technique to use first thing in the morning when you get up. Instead of asking why you have to get up, or how you are going to survive the day, or why you have to suffer through another Monday, or any of the usual disempowering questions that people use to get their day off to a rotten start, you can use questions from your own list.

Remember, your brain is going to give you an answer to the question you ask it. Let me tell you, if you get in the habit of asking yourself questions like "How can I be more enthusiastic?" as opposed to "Why do I have to do this stupid stuff?," you will experience states that will be so far superior to the ones that came with the negative questions that you will cringe every time you hear those negative questions coming from yourself or from others.

Gratitude is an Invaluable Aid to a Positive State

As you can see, state has a lot to do with attitude, and we all know how much fun it is to be around someone who has a habitually negative attitude (especially if that someone is ourself!) As a closing note, I want to share with you one of the best aids that I know of for opening ourselves up to empowering and resourceful states, a concept that serves us as well as *any* we could develop. I'm talking about developing an attitude of gratitude.

We don't hear much about gratitude anymore, but that certainly isn't to our advantage. It seems that the majority of people, mostly interested in what they can get, are generally miserable because they don't have it, and disappointed when they do get it because then they want something else. Not exactly a recipe for happiness is it? Well, just like you learned in kindergarten: Just because everybody's doing it, it doesn't make it right! What's missing from this state of affairs that most people get locked into is a healthy grounding in gratitude. How many people are actually thankful for what they *do* have? How many people even stop to think about what they *do* have? Do you?

A lot of this ingratitude is not hard to understand, seeing as how we are constantly bombarded with reasons for dissatisfaction. Let's face it--the main role of advertising in general is to leave you feeling incomplete unless you have the particular item that the commercial is telling you to buy, regardless of how useless the thing might be. We want the things that others have, so we are dissatisfied. We want to *be* what others are, so we are dissatisfied. If it isn't *something else*, we don't want it!

The Stonecutter

Despite all of the people telling us that times have changed, this failure to appreciate what we have or where we are isn't a new condition. In fact, there's another ancient Chinese story which sums it up perfectly--the story of the stonecutter: Once, there was a stonecutter, and he wasn't happy with his position in life or what he had accomplished thus far.

Upon passing a rich merchant's house one day, he looked in and saw the exquisite furnishings and influential visitors. "If only I were a wealthy merchant," thought the stonecutter, angrily, "I could live like this and wouldn't have to be a lowly stonecutter."

To his astonishment, his wish was instantly granted and he became a merchant, more wealthy and powerful than the one he had envied. Now, *he* was envied and hated by those who were less powerful than he, and this made him glad.

But then he heard a commotion and saw a government official being carried through the streets on a sedan chair escorted by soldiers. Regardless of how wealthy they were, everyone had to bow down as the official's entourage passed. "What if I were a government official? Then, everyone would have to bow down to me!"

Suddenly, he became a powerful government official with an even larger entourage. Now, he was being carried around the streets of the town in a lavishly decorated sedan chair while the people bowed low in envy and fear. But it was a very hot day, and the official began sweating heavily. In his discomfort, he glanced at the sun and cursed his tormentor, which just shone steadily, unaffected by the official or his procession. "If I could be the sun, then I would be powerful, indeed!"

Lo and behold, without warning, he became the sun. Now, he was shining furiously upon the town and wilting the crops in the fields. Townspeople and countryfolk, lord and peasant alike, swore at him with raised fists, but to no avail. All of a sudden, however, a great dark cloud came between him and the earth, and he could no longer menace the people below. "This storm cloud is more powerful than I. If I were a storm cloud, I could rain down upon the land!"

Now he was a storm cloud, loosing his fury. Great torrents of rain flooded the land, and the people cursed him mightily. But, then he found that he was being moved along by a great gust of wind. "I cannot believe the power of this wind," he thought. "If I were the wind there would be no limit to my might!"

And so it happened--he was the wind. And, oh, how he blew down upon the land. Trees were cast down, houses were blown over--none could stand his fury, and all were afraid and hated him! However, there was one thing that could resist his onslaught. Alone in a field stood a gigantic boulder, towering above the countryside. It would not be harmed, no matter how hard he blew! "Oh, if I could be this mighty rock, nothing could avail against me!"

So, he was the boulder, the lord of the countryside. There he sat, proud and powerful, until a day came when he heard one clink and then another, like a hammer and chisel, and he realized he was losing something of his power. "What is going on here?," he demanded. But the hammering continued, regardless of this protest. Suddenly frightened, he looked down. There below him was a humble stonecutter, whistling contentedly as he chiseled.

If You Don't Appreciate What You Have Now, Why Will You Appreciate it Later?

How often are we like the stonecutter? It's so easy to be dissatisfied with what we have, given all the avenues of disenchantment that are there for us to walk along. But, if we want to be happy, we've got to learn to appreciate that which we have within our grasp before we reach for something else. Gratitude is an essential ingredient to a positive state. When you begin to habitually look at your life in terms of how fortunate you are, a whole new world emerges. This is reframing at its most basic, and the rewards are many.

We take so much for granted on a daily basis that it's embarrassing. But we don't have to be this way. All it takes is a quick look around us to see what we are blessed to have. Look at how much of the stuff that we never bother to stop and think about is lacking in the lives of other folks. The basics of food, clothing, and shelter are denied to so many, and yet, there we are, warm and cared for, bellies full and bitching.

Of course, the point isn't for us to feel guilty about what we have or that we might want to do even better. After all, this book is dedicated to helping improve your resources, your skills, and your situation. It's not wrong to want things to be better than they are, but it *is* wrong not to appreciate what you have while you continue striving to accomplish your pursuits. And the reason why it *is* wrong is that if you are not grateful for what you have now there's little chance that you will appreciate what you have later.

Nothing is enough to the man
for whom enough is too little.
--Epicurus

People often believe that if they could only get _____,
then they would be happy. This is one of the biggest fallacies that
we can fall into. Our happiness and fulfillment *do not* depend on
acquiring that "something else." If you truly want to succeed, you
must learn to be grateful for what you have now. You've got to
understand that history is filled with men and women who
seemingly had *everything* that a person could desire, and yet they
were still miserable. They had never learned to be grateful. It
always comes down to state. If you can't learn the necessity of
developing a grateful state, why do you think a bunch of *stuff*, or
different circumstances is going to make you happier than you are
now? All of us get into situations that we wish would just go
away. Let's be honest--that algebra class or English class that is
such torture for you is quite possibly being taught by someone
who wishes more than anything that they didn't have to deal with
so many people like *you* every day.

How to Be Grateful? I'm Glad You Asked

So, how do you learn to be appreciative, to work from a basic
state of gratitude? It's simple. Like I said earlier, just ask. Your
brain will give you many reasons if you sincerely ask, "What do
I have to be grateful for?" "How can I be more grateful?" is also
a great question to get in the habit of asking on a daily basis.
There truly is so much we have to be thankful for, and the more
we learn to appreciate what we have, the more we are able to
appreciate what we will receive in the future.

But, if we fail to appreciate what we've got *now,* we stand little
chance of feeling better about what comes along later because our
focus will already be trained on the negative. Think about it.
Since any new situation will always have negative aspects to it,

our negative focus will lock onto them, and we will be in that miserable state, saying, "Ok, this is almost pretty good, but what I *really* want is . . . " Is that where you perpetually want to be? If not, look at your life and work on focusing on the things that you have to be grateful for. And don't lose sight of them as you strive to gain more.

Look at your family. Look at your friends. It's easy to find things wrong with these situations, but ask yourself if you would remove these people with a snap of your fingers if you could. (If not, look to see what is positive and focus on that. If yes, then ask yourself why and see what you can do to make things better, because these people are in your life for a reason.)

Look at your goals and realize how fortunate you are to even *have* specific goals. Most people don't even understand the need for them. Look at your classes and see what it is that you can gain from them, what skills you can acquire in order to help you reach your goals. What's good about where you live or where you work? What's going on in your community? What about your spiritual life? Have you looked into these things?

It's easy to dismiss all of these examples and say that there's nothing good about any of this stuff, but only in the most extreme cases is this actually true. And, even if you *are* in one of those extreme cases, you are still learning valuable skills to improve your situation right now. Yes, folks, I humbly submit that you should be grateful to have this book. After all, most people don't know anything about this stuff, let alone have access to it. And *you* are getting it at an early stage in your development, and you can reap amazing results if you apply yourself. You have *much* to be grateful for. Find it, and focus on it!

You see, it's kind of like a cosmic law: Those that appreciate what they have acquire even more to appreciate, while those who don't appreciate what they have, won't appreciate what they have, whatever it is. Don't be one of these unfortunate people. Be grateful. Ask yourself what you have to be grateful for, and how you can be more grateful. Do this every day and you will develop a habit that will allow you to reap benefits that you never dreamed were possible. And you can't imagine how good it feels.

As you now know, state is the key to how you feel and state is determined by your reaction to, or associations regarding, the events and circumstances of the outside world. Since *you* determine your state (by continual interactions between your posture and your internal representations), it is in your best interest to manage your state by learning how to habitually access resourceful, empowering states instead of negative, disempowering ones. The choice *is* yours and you now have a number of proven tools to work with. It's time to put them all together and begin to accomplish the dreams and goals that you want.

Chapter Eight

Putting It All Together

All right, you've got all of the tools, but it's been a while since you've been dealing with some of them. So, let's put the all of the techniques together in a review that will help you see the whole picture. To do this effectively, I want to create a focus, or foundation upon which to hang them so that you may see how they work together and reinforce each other to make an unbeatable total package. (This review will necessarily be concentrated. The techniques are presented in the same order here as they were before, with the only exception being that this review starts with goals. If you get confused about anything, look it up in the original chapter for more detail.)

I've said over and over that these techniques can be used, and have been used, to achieve success in many different areas. But, the primary area that this book is concerned with is your success in school. And, whether we like it or not, the main measuring stick for success in school is still your report card. I know it's not always an accurate measurement of intelligence, achievement, or learning, and I know that there are many people who agree with me on this opinion. You might be one.

But, it makes no difference whether or not we are right or wrong, because it doesn't change the fact that, like it or not, your report card is what is going to represent you in the eyes of people who are going to have a direct impact on your life, even if you never meet them or find out who they are. You aren't going to get a chance to explain why those D's in English, or those C's in math weren't fair, or accurate, or justified. So, regardless of how you feel about report cards, why not learn to get good ones. After all, I've never heard anyone argue against, or try to justify their report card when it had straight A's on it. So let's do it. Let's see how the different techniques work together towards achieving the goal of straight A's.

Straight A's: A Perfectly Clear and Specific Goal

The first step is easy because you already have your goal: You are going to get straight A's on your next report card. (Of course, if you are in the middle of a quarter or semester when you begin this work, and it is already too late to get these grades, your goal will be to get them on the report card following the next one. But don't wait until then to get to work!) Initially, this is a frightening statement for most people to make because it is direct and clear and there's no room for misinterpretation. Either you are going to have straight A's or you're not, and most people seem to like things a little more vague than that. But, now you know better. You are going to have a far better chance of achieving your goal because *you* are not going to wait for it to sneak up on you. You are going to plan for it.

The great thing about this goal of straight A's is its ability to keep you on track. You know *exactly* what you are shooting for, and you will immediately know if you begin deviating. If you remember the study that I talked about that was done at Yale University in 1953 concerning goals, you will remember that the students that had specific, written goals and a plan to achieve them wound up being worth more than the other 97% combined!

Your Goal Gives You Drive and Motivation

Remember, goals drive your actions. When you have a definite, specific direction in which you are moving, you are able to see past temporary obstacles by keeping your eyes on your goal. Without your goal of straight A's, every little problem that comes up can become a major distraction, because without the direction that your A's provide, the problems are often all that you can see. With your A's as a goal, you don't have to get caught up in the problems that most students face when they don't like either the subject, the class, or the teacher. Instead of getting bogged down in these distractions which have nothing to do with achieving your goal, you are guided by it and move right past the stuff that prevents others from getting good grades.

Your goal will also help to keep you motivated. Let's face it: Just because you have a specific direction you are heading in and you have a workable plan to achieve it, doesn't mean that every step of the way is going to be easy or fun. But people with specific goals find that having a definite direction to move in lets them focus on the ultimate result and push through the difficult times and distractions. So, now *being* one of these people, you can start to build up momentum, allowing the whole process to become easier.

Also, this momentum is valuable in helping you to keep going when things get difficult or start going wrong because, unlike someone without a specific goal, you won't get sidetracked or discouraged by things going haywire. For example, say you screw up on a test. Instead of moaning about it and feeling defeated, your goal to get straight A's forces you to move ahead and make the adjustments which will insure that you don't mess up on the next test.

Goal Guidelines

As you remember from the goal chapter, there are steps to take to insure your goal stays prominent in your focus. The first is to write down in detail your goal and a plan for its accomplishment. Since you already know your goal, you might be tempted to skip this part. But remember, by being unwilling to commit your goal to writing, you are sending a message to your brain that you are not truly serious about accomplishing it. So, write it down in big letters: I WILL GET STRAIGHT A's ON MY NEXT REPORT CARD.

Now that you have the goal that you are committed to pursuing, begin writing a goal plan. Writing things down forces you to concentrate more on what you are doing, and it also shows you quickly how vague your ideas can be. Often, people think that they know just what they are going to do, but when they try to write their plans down, they realize that they can't get a clear handle on what they are doing. If you can't write it down in a clear manner, you need to think it out more thoroughly, Of course, you don't need every detail of your plan firmly in place before you begin. But you need some plan in order to know how to get what you're are going after.

Check out the goal plan guidelines in Chapter Four for detailed information on how to develop a plan for your goal. Write down as much detail as you can come up with because the clearer the picture your brain has, the more compelled it will be to move in the direction of your goal.

Of course, you are not locked into your plan if you realize that changes are necessary. If, as you move ahead, you see things that you didn't consider initially, make the necessary adjustments and keep on working.

Having straight A's as your goal meets the requirements which are necessary for the next four steps of the goal process: Your goal is stated in the positive (straight A's), your goal is something you can control (they're *your* grades), you can tell when you have accomplished your goal (your report card), and you have a timeline for the accomplishment of your goal (the end of the grading period).

As I emphasized in the goal chapter, just because you don't know at first how you are going to accomplish straight A's doesn't mean you shouldn't pursue them. If you do have a clear idea of how to go about getting them, fine. But it isn't necessary to have everything figured out before you get going. (If it was necessary, I wouldn't have even *started* writing this book yet, because I had to figure out all kinds of things as I went along.)

Your Straight A Identity

Now that you have a clear-cut goal and have worked out a plan which is as detailed as you can make it at this time, you have the necessary direction needed to make true progress. Your next step is to begin working on your straight A student identity. This is necessary because, as you've learned, changes on the outside do not stick unless you make the necessary changes in identity on the inside. Before anything else, it is how you *see* yourself that will determine the level at which you perform.

Do You *Expect* to Get Straight A's?

It's not always the smartest students, or the hardest working students who get the best grades. The students who get A's are the students who *expect* to get straight A's. This isn't a matter of being cocky or of lying to yourself. It's a matter of commitment. You are committed to your goal, so you know that you are going to do the necessary work (with the necessary attitude) to get the job done. Identity is the key for anyone who produces consistent results. Your identity *must* be that of an A student because of your inherent interest in being right. If you see yourself as an A student, your brain will operate in the necessary ways to make your results go along with your identity.

Traits of a Straight A Student

So, the question you need to answer is. What are the traits that make up an A student? Although no two students are the same, there are certain similarities that A students seem to share. (Obviously, there are always going to be exceptions, but we don't want to worry about them here.)

Prepared, Ready to Go, and Paying Attention

A students generally come to class every day. Many students may do this, but A students have an *attitude* about it; they come to class on time, with paper, pen or pencil, and the required text and/or assignment. And, they are ready to go. A students pay attention to what the teacher is saying, even when they don't like the subject, the teacher, or the class. If something important comes up, they catch it right away.

Write Down Assignments
and Don't Be Afraid to Ask Questions

A students write down all of their assignments (as well as the directions that go along with them) right away. They *don't* pretend that they will remember it later. So get yourself a notebook or planner so that you can keep all of your assignments straight and in one place.

If there is something that is unclear about an assignment, the A student will ask about it right away. I am always hearing students say that they don't ask questions because they have teachers who won't answer their questions. If this is true, I am sure that there is something wrong with the communication between the teacher and student. Somewhere along the way, something broke down, and it hasn't been addressed. Trust me, if you are sincere in your efforts to do well, your teacher will pick up on it, and he or she will help you, even if the two of you have had problems in the past. Like I said before, teachers are happy to help students who truly want that help because teachers don't get a lot of this kind of interaction. You can be sure that after dealing all day with students who don't care, a teacher will appreciate the few students who *do* care. If you are one of the students, you will be recognized for it.

Participate Actively

An A student readily participates in class, either in giving answers, or in asking productive questions. This isn't a matter of kissing up or trying to look good. A students know that participating in the process makes it easier to learn and, if worse comes to worse, makes the time go by faster. Actively working in class is far better than passively sitting there wondering if it will ever be over because passivity is the best way to not learn something. It's true that there are often A students who don't talk much in class, but they don't just sit there like lumps. They are active on the inside, interacting with the material in a positive way because it makes the learning more effective.

Don't Waste Time

A students don't waste a lot of time. If there are study periods or times during class when there is free time, A students don't spend it socializing if there is work to be done. It's kind of funny that the kids who whine the most about not having enough time are the ones who don't intelligently use the time they *do* have. A students know their friends aren't going to hate them if they get their work done instead of talking. Not having enough time is a major complaint these days, and it's true that we do have busy lives, but most of the time, it's just an excuse. If you look around, there are always some people who get all kinds of things done in the same time most others use to sit around and complain about the fact that they have no time. It's like the old saying, "everybody gets the same twenty-four hours in a day." If you take a close look at how you are spending your time, you will see that much of it is probably being wasted. A students have developed habits that get the most out of the same twenty-four hours.

No Whining, Please

A students don't complain. (And, oh, how I thank them for that!) Do you know how much time and energy most students waste in complaining about things that are going to happen anyway? This seems like a harmless way of blowing off steam, especially before a test or an essay or some other project, but there's more to it than that. Constant complaining affects your state. If your brain receives messages of complaint, it tends to adopt that attitude. So, even if you don't really mean it, you have to fight your way out of that negative state before you can get down to business. Many students aren't that successful at shifting their state, so they get stuck working from this complaining state and produce results that go along with it. Rotten results. There's a better way, and A students know it. If you have a habit of whining about assignments (and most students do) get to work breaking it. The easiest way to begin is to just keep your mouth shut when assignments are given and don't pay attention to, or chime in with, other students who do complain. Believe me, they won't notice that you aren't playing along.

These are some key elements that go into the identity of an A student, and they are ones which you should work on if you are serious about becoming an A student in identity. Of course, since you are committed to doing so, and you now *expect* to be an A student, you have to make sure your beliefs support your expectations. After all, it's no good saying "I expect to get straight A's" and have that little voice in your head whisper back to you, "No, you don't!"

Beliefs Make Up Your Identity

When I compared identity to a building, I said that beliefs are the bricks that make it up and that they are practically the most important element in shaping our lives because they shape the way we perceive the world. And now, it is your job to reach the point where you truly *believe* that you are an A student. A belief is a sense of certainty, a sense of "this is the way it is." Beliefs act as filters between you and the outside world, and the beliefs you have will direct the results you get. If you want to have the identity of an A student, you will have to program in the beliefs that you *are* an A student.

If You Don't Believe You Can Get Straight A's, You are Absolutely Right

I've mentioned several times already how often we get stuck in notions of "being realistic," and that this silly notion only seems to come up when someone wants to argue for their limitations or your limitations. And I've always countered this idea with the argument that it doesn't matter whether or not a belief is based in reality. Remember the story of the way they train elephants in India? If a mighty elephant believes it cannot break a rope that in reality it could snap in a second, it's absolutely right--it can't! Well, we're just like elephants because we often operate under false beliefs, beliefs formed long ago which we have allowed to shape our lives in limiting ways. Not all cages have bars.

If you don't currently believe that you are an A student, you are correct. But, remember, it is your beliefs that control how much of your resources you will use in any given situation. Maybe you are like the elephant, convinced that you can't break the rope. You aren't going to know unless you step out of your limiting beliefs and begin programming new, empowering ones because your brain will direct your behavior in the direction of your belief. Your brain is quite efficient; it gives you exactly what you put into it on a consistent basis, so what do you think might happen if you consistently believe that you are an A student?

Of Course, You Need to Practice

It's not going to just happen; you're going to have to work at it. You see, beliefs are just like anything else--they are reinforced through conditioning, or practice. You are going to learn to believe that you are an A student. And, how do you learn how to do anything? Through repetition, right? Do something over and over and it becomes second nature.

Think of the example I gave about tying your shoelaces. If you'll remember, the repetition of an action establishes pathways in your nervous system which are called neural pathways. The more established these pathways become, the more "automatic" an action or behavior becomes. At first, just like learning to tie your shoelaces the opposite way than you normally do, your work with believing that you are an A student will be clumsy, and you will have to pay a lot of attention to what you are doing. But, after awhile, as you keep working with the idea, it will begin to feel natural. Soon, you won't be thinking about it at all. It will just be the way it is. You *are* an A student.

Belief Guidelines

So. Here's a quick rundown on how to do it. (The detailed version is in the chapter on beliefs. Check it out.)

Step One: Decide that you *must* change your disempowering belief.

This is important because if you don't feel that you must change this belief, you won't be motivated to actually work on changing, and you will fall back into your old patterns when the novelty of the new idea wears off. (And don't worry, it will.) Straight A's is a great idea until the work begins. Then, you might find other things to do. Thankfully, there's step two.

Step Two: Attach real pain to the old belief.

You need to understand, and *feel*, specifically, and in detail, what your old belief will cost you now and in the future if you don't change it. What's the belief that you can't get straight A's going to bring you? Don't just say "that's bad!" Write out in detail what this rotten little belief is doing to your ability to succeed. What results are you going to miss out on if you stay with this baby elephant of a belief?

Step Three: Attach great pleasure to your new, empowering belief.

If you are going to move away from your old, limiting, painful belief, you need something to move towards. What are the benefits of getting straight A's? Oh, c'mon, you can probably think of a few. Write out in detail all of the benefits that you will gain by adopting this new belief and making it part of your identity. Now, look at your list from your disempowering belief side by side with your list from your empowering belief. Which path looks more attractive to you? Which one do you want to head down? The choice really *is* yours.

Step Four: Install the A student belief into your brain's computer.

Yes, this brings us to the concept of producing your desired results in advance. So let's not waste any time.

Imaging Your Straight A's

Straight A's, straight A's, *you* have gotten straight A's. How does it feel? *Success is not an accident!* Successful people in *all* fields share the ability to see themselves achieving their goals *before* they set out to accomplish them. Successful people have habits of success, and this attribute of getting results in advance is one of them.

Imaging works because your brain responds to strongly imagined ideas and moves you in the direction they provide. By conditioning your mind for straight A's, you will reach the point where you *expect* to get straight A's, the point where you need to be in order to get straight A's.

Everybody Images

People attempting to shoot down the idea of imaging like to point to the "real" world, saying that that's where it really matters. Well, no kidding. But, these people overlook a simple fact. There isn't **anything** that's been created in the "real" world that hasn't first been **imagined** in the mind. And our thoughts generally fall into habitual patterns. Since successful people expect successful results and spend their mental effort imaging successful results in advance, they generally produce these results. They're using the same technique as the unsuccessful people are using, but they are pointing it in a positive direction instead of a negative one. Now that you are committed to moving in the positive direction of getting straight A's, you can benefit from the same habit of imaging that other successful people use.

Imaging for A's

So how do you practice imaging for straight A's? (You might want to review the practice procedure laid out in Chapter Three before proceeding.) Take your new belief ("I am a straight A student") and think of a situation where it would apply. The most obvious one, and one you should definitely work on, is when you receive your next report card. See yourself bringing home a report card with straight A's. *Your* straight A's. How does it feel to hand a report card like this to your parents? How does it feel to know that your hard work has brought you another success? How does it feel for your parents and *you* to be proud of you? Feel these positive feelings deeply. The success and the pride that come with these A's are the result of the fact that you are a hard worker, that *you* are a success. *You* did this! Feel the confidence that comes from such an effort, confidence that you can apply to any area that you choose because hard work in one area translates to hard work in any other area. After all, you *are* an A student, and the good habits that go with getting straight A's will work for you in any other pursuit as well. Realize that you are building a foundation for success throughout your life. Savor how good this success will feel. Get it so that you can taste it.

Repeat this process for a couple of minutes daily, using different situations and emphasizing the fact that you *are* an A student. See yourself receiving an assignment and tackling it immediately and with gusto, because that's how an A student does it. See yourself taking a test and knowing you are going to get an A on it because you are obviously prepared and are confident that you will be successful. The more you work with your imaging, the better you get at it, and the better you get at it, the better your results.

Watching the Imaging Seeds Grow

Remember, repeating an action over and over again sets up neural pathways in your nervous system, and your brain doesn't know the difference between your getting A's for real and your strongly imagining yourself getting them. So, if you work with concentration and feeling (just like so many great athletes and other professionals do), you are mentally training, and this mental repetition will greatly assist you in your actually getting straight A's because it will strongly reinforce your straight A identity.

Imaging is like planting seeds. By planting positive, deliberate images of your success in your mind, you are preparing yourself for a successful harvest. Of course, this isn't magic. You still have to do the work along the way, just as you do when you plant a garden. But, if you are consistently working on your belief in your imagination, you will see that you are getting much better results in the "real" world as well. As you build up momentum, you will get more and more evidence for your new belief. Soon, you won't have to consciously work on it; it will be a stable part of who you are. Imagine how good that feels!

You Want It, You Got It

Your focus is simply what you are paying attention to at any given moment. It doesn't sound like a big deal, but, ultimately, *the quality of your life is directly determined by your focus.* So, now that you are committed to being an A student, what do you think your focus should be on? Most people don't even think about it; they just follow their habitual patterns of focus. Of course, by now, *you* are no longer the average person. (If you were, you wouldn't have gotten this far, and you wouldn't be interested in taking these positive steps which, admittedly, *do* eliminate the excuses, but, happily, *replace* them with success.)

In the chapter on focus, we looked at an average school day from a negatively focused standpoint and found that from that viewpoint everything about school sucked. It's an easy focus to have, but that doesn't mean that you want it because *you get what you focus on*. If you go looking for it, you're probably going to find it. If you focus on it, that's what you are going to see.

You Don't Want It, Stop *Looking* for It

So, obviously, if you are going to get straight A's, you are going to need a positive focus. But having a positive focus doesn't mean just telling yourself that everything is wonderful, that everything about school, teachers, and homework is the absolute best! Remember, since you can't consciously take in everything going on around you or within you, you are always focusing on only a portion of the picture. But what portion you *do* focus on is up to you. If you don't want to see the worst in every situation, stop looking for it. That's the first, and biggest step.

Shifting your focus does *not* mean pretending things are different than they really are. If you were previously looking at things from a "school sucks" focus, that was no more real than your new "what do I need to focus on to get straight A's" approach. Whatever you choose to focus on *becomes* your reality because you are going to see the whole picture from that angle. It's like the Super Bowl. In the same game there's a winner and a loser. But, just because the losing team feels horrible, it doesn't mean that the winning team's celebration isn't real.

It's not that easy to change your focus just like that. If you've been working from a negative standpoint, you've had lot's of time to program that pattern into your brain. It isn't going to change just because you wake up one day and say "I'm going to see everything from a straight A student's point of view!" You're going to need to keep on top of your thought patterns. Luckily, you are now working with extra tools to make your job easier. So, instead of trying to change your focus all by itself, link your new focus to your straight A identity, your straight A beliefs, and your straight A goal. This makes your task easier, since all parts of your overall success program are working together, thus creating the ever-desired momentum.

For Fun, Focus on the Goal

Now that you know that your focus is on doing what is needed for getting straight A's, instead of getting bogged down in whether or not you like the teacher or the assignment, your focus is on your goal. Therefore, you jump on the assignment right away. Since you are committed to achieving your goal, *it* becomes the most important part of the equation, not how you feel about geometry or vocabulary, etc. Now, instead of experiencing misery every time you get an assignment, you enjoy it because you are anticipating getting an A on it, and that feels good. By doing well on the assignment, you are naturally prepared for the test, so you'll most likely get an A on that, too. And, you don't have to waste any time talking yourself into liking the assignment, the class, or the teacher, because your success has *nothing* to do with any of them. You *do* have to talk yourself into liking A's. Do you think that's going to be a problem?

Focus, and Let Your RAS Do Its Job

In the chapter on focus, I said that once you know your goal, you should focus on it and get started working towards it right away, even if you don't know how you were going to accomplish it. Now, even though you've been exposed to some useful strategies, maybe you feel that you don't know everything you should in order to get straight A's. If this is so, don't let it stop you. If you keep focused and move ahead, doors *will* open up for you, revealing needed information or resources to help you on your way. Remember the reticular activating system? The RAS's function is to determine what you pay attention to, and your focus is what triggers it. When you focus on your goal of getting straight A's, it becomes important to you, and your RAS will alert you to anything related to it. Since *you get what you focus on*, if you are serious and keep focusing on getting straight A's, you will find information and resources to help you achieve them. So, don't wait for all of the answers before you begin. Let your RAS do its job. It's an important part of focus, and your focus can dramatically change the quality of the results you achieve.

Associations are the Key to State

The final technique in our armory is state. State is the key to your ability, as well as your inability, to perform at the levels necessary to be successful because your behavior in any given situation is going to be influenced far more by your state than by anything happening on the outside. Remember, it's not the homework that you hate, and it's not the tests that you hate, it's the *associations*. *Your state is determined by what you associate with the things that happen to you, not the things themselves.*

If you associate a bunch of negative baggage with tests, for example, it's the associations that you don't like, not the tests. So, if you want to change the way you feel about something, change the associations you link to it. Focus on the positive aspects of it (here's another chance to get an A) and your state will change towards the positive because your brain just follows the directions that you give it. If you want to consistently succeed, you've got to learn to take control of, or manage, your state.

Your Posture Will Follow the Directions You Give It

One of the major factors determining state is your posture, or the way you use your body. Your brain and your body work together to determine how you feel. If you habitually adopt a posture of depression or tiredness, your brain will act upon the signals it receives from your body and respond accordingly. As I've been saying all along, your brain is like a computer in that it runs whatever program you load into it. If, by your posture, you load a program which tells the brain that you feel tired, then the brain will accept the information and provide you with reasons to be tired. And you *will* feel tired. Of course, if you load in a program that has you feeling filled with energy, you *will* feel energized.

That's right, just act *as if* you were filled with energy. Move your body *as if* you were totally pumped with energy. Breath deeply like you do when you are filled with energy. *Be* like you would be if you were filled with energy and enthusiasm. If you do this with sincerity, you will definitely receive more energy and feel enthusiastic, because your body will be sending the same signals as those which are present when you are normally enthusiastic and energetic. Your brain will then interpret them to mean that you *are* enthusiastic and energetic and respond accordingly--even if only moments ago you were sending signals to your brain which said you were tired.

Don't even say that this is only pretending to be energetic when you're really tired. By now, you know the answer! *It doesn't matter which state is "real" because your brain acts on the data it receives, regardless of whether it is "real" or not.* Your reality is shaped by your beliefs. If you believe that you are tired, you will feel tired. If you believe that you are filled with energy, you aren't going to feel tired.

Walk Like You Have A's in Your Pockets

What you want to do is consciously use your body to reflect the states of energy, enthusiasm, and success that are necessary for your achievement of straight A's. Now, maybe it's hard for you to believe that your *body* could have anything to do with getting A's. After all, A's are a mental thing, right? But there *is* a connection. Remember, it all has to do with success. Although you are learning skills that can, and have, been applied to every area of success, *your* focus is on getting A's. Therefore, your posture of success is directed towards getting A's. When you are no longer in school, you will be using this same stuff to accomplish things in other areas. But, until then . . .

You want to move with confidence. Look at the successful person's walk. Isn't it true that successful people seem to walk as if they've got somewhere to be, as if they have a purpose? It's a deliberateness instead of an aimlessness, and there is power in their stride. It's not an in-your-face kind of attitude, but one that is dignified, one that is respected and respectful.

As it is with walking, so it is with sitting and standing. You want to carry yourself with deliberateness, with authority. Sit up straight and stand up straight. It *does* make a difference. When you are consistently slouched over and looking as if you are about to fall asleep, you send messages to your brain and to other people that you aren't operating at full speed.

Sending Signals for Success

So practice your straight A posture. When you do, you will feel a surge of confidence and energy. And remember, it *isn't* fake. You feel it is because you are sending signals of confidence and energy to your brain, and it is responding by sending back the same feelings that those who are already successful feel, which is why *they* carry themselves the way they do. Take advantage of the loop that is created between body and mind: The more you use your body to create a positive state, the more positive your state will be, and the more positive your state, the more you will use your body to maintain that state.

Being tired or not feeling well are two of the most prevalent excuses students use when they aren't doing as well as they know they could be doing, and they are excuses that are *so* easy to overcome. You don't have to fall into the trap that so many students (and other people) fall prey to. You're an A student now. Use your body accordingly.

In What Direction are Your Self-Talk Patterns Taking You?

While posture plays a major part in state, it is only half of the story. Obviously, your mind plays a critical part in determining how you feel, and it does so in two major ways. Much of your state comes from what you *say* to yourself and how you represent, or *picture* things in your mind.

Self-talk is that ever-present dialogue that you are having with yourself. It's important because you use it to make sense of the world. Your conclusions about the way things are come from decisions you make during these conversations with yourself.

Possible problems enter when you fall into habitual patterns with your self-talk. These patterns can be hazardous if they are made up of negative messages because your brain doesn't stop and say, "Hey, this isn't right. This isn't true." As you certainly are aware of by now, whether or not these self-talk beliefs are actually true or not makes no difference whatsoever. If you believe that that's the way it is, then *that's* the way it is! What programs are you playing day after day, week after week, year after year? The programs that you continually play determine the direction in which you will be moving.

You Can Change Your Self-Talk *IF* You Want to

The key to changing your negative self-talk programs is just that-- change them! What you want to do is to *replace* the old, negative program with a more consciously directed positive program. Again, it's just like beliefs: If you are running a program that says "I'm lazy and can't get my work done," you need to *consciously* and *consistently* replace it with the opposite program that you would rather have: "I'm an A student who does what's needed to get my work done."

Of course, if I suggest doing something like changing your programs, there is a part of you that is going to say, "Hey I can't do that; it's a lie. I really *am* lazy." (Ok, this must be the 37th time I've brought up this point. But, one more time might finally get it through, so one more time it is.) If "I'm lazy" is a program that you consistently run, then lazy it is, and lazy *you* are because your reality is what you believe it to be. But, talking yourself into your state is all that you've done, and you can talk yourself out of it, too. You just have to be willing to work at it. There's no rule that says you have to stay the way you believe yourself to be right now. If you *want* to change, you *can* change. If you change your state, *reality* has a way of changing right along with it.

Self-Talking Yourself Into Straight A's
Also, if the idea of working with your self-talk programs seems strange, remember that *you are already doing it*! You are not learning how to do anything new here. You are just taking *conscious* control of something you've been doing all of your life.

So, how do you self-talk you way to straight A's?

Step One: Find any negative programs that you want to replace.
A good way to spot a negative program is to take your goal of straight A's and ask yourself, "What could possibly get in the way of my accomplishing this goal?" If there are negative programs connected with your A's, they will probably make themselves known as objections, fears, or reservations.

Step Two: Replace the negative programs with positive ones.
This one's easy, huh? "I am an A student." "I do the necessary work to get A's." "By being prepared, I get A's on all of my tests." "Because I am focused, getting A's comes naturally to me." There are many variations you can use, so use a bunch of

them.

As with identity, beliefs, and imaging, don't worry if you don't feel that you are actually behaving in this way at the moment. Your previous self-talk has put limits on your behavior, and these limits are going to have to be removed. By consistently focusing on your new program of being an A student, you will begin to see definite changes in your behavior, and these changes will reinforce your belief that you *are* an A student. As you continue to work, you will see a positive loop form just as with your posture: positive self-talk creates positive results and positive results create more positive self-talk.

Step Three: Be consistent in your practice.

Like everything else, the more you practice, the better you get. Replacing negative programs that may have been running for years isn't going to happen with just one or two attempts. You've got to keep at it. Again, you are fortunate to be doing this work in conjunction with the other techniques.

Step Four: Find a regular time to practice.

First thing in the morning and before you go to bed are excellent times to work at this, but you can do it anytime that is comfortable for you. Just make sure that you are as consistent as possible because we are creatures of habit.

Speaking of habits, don't forget about homeostasis, the tendency of a system to resist changes or disruptions. It's another reason to be consistent in your practice because then you can use it to your benefit. After adjusting to the initial shock to the system that your new program of straight A's might produce, homeostasis will help you accomplish your goal. Instead of continuing to play the negative programs and wondering why you aren't getting anywhere, be consistent with the programming of your positive self-talk and you will find yourself working from a positive, resourceful state with greater frequency than you thought was possible.

Reframing is Critical for Turning Setbacks Into Successes

Along with self-talk, another important element in creating state is the way you represent, or picture things to yourself. As I've said, *your state is determined by what you associate to the things that happen to you, NOT the things themselves.* These associations make up the frame through which you see the picture of the event. Change the frame, and you can change the way you feel about things. This is *reframing*, and it is critical to your consistent and continued success with all of the tools you have learned to work with, whether identity, beliefs, imaging, goals, or focus. You need to be able to see your circumstances in the most positive light.

Reframing is invaluable when you've made a mistake, like blowing a test or screwing up an assignment. Normally, when we look back on mistakes, we get upset or feel embarrassed about it. But, reframing allows you to look at a situation or circumstance and see what can be gained from it to help you succeed in your goals. Instead of whining about screwing up, or looking for some reason why it couldn't have been *your* fault, reframe the situation and find out what happened. Then, when you find the problem, you can work to make sure you don't repeat it. Coming up with a valuable piece of information to increase your efficiency in the future is definitely worth a mistake here and there, and reframing is the way to do it. After all, we are far more likely to pay attention when we screw up than when we are cruising along successfully.

Just Ask for What You Need

Yet another oh, so simple way to change your state is to just ask. That's right, just ask your brain and it will show you how. When you get in a situation that you normally don't care for, like an

English or math class or something, just pose some questions: "How can I have a better focus here?" "How can I improve my state?" "What can I do to stay on task to get my A?" If you really want to do it, and aren't just asking half-heartedly, your brain will show you an angle that you hadn't considered before. Get in the habit of asking questions that lead your brain to come up with these reasons, and do it on a daily basis. The more you do it, the easier it becomes and the stronger your habit of accessing positive states becomes.

Along the same lines, you can also make a list of characteristics that you think would be valuable for an A student like yourself to have. Then, with concentration, ask yourself, "How can I be more _____?" Your brain will focus on these characteristics and lead you in those directions by putting you in a state which is conducive to these characteristics.

Gratitude is the Attitude

Regardless of how hard you work with these techniques, sometimes, things are going to go wrong. Because you are working so hard, it's easy to get discouraged. During these times, it's necessary to remember the importance of gratitude. You don't want to lose sight of what you are doing well, of what *is* going right. Gratitude is an excellent attitude to develop because it is such an effective way to keep your state positive. When you begin to habitually look at your life in terms of how fortunate you are, a whole new world emerges. This is reframing at its most basic and the rewards have to be felt to be believed.

If you want to work from a basic state of gratitude, just ask "what do I have to be grateful for?" If you are sincere, your brain will give you plenty of reasons. "How can I be more grateful?" is also a great question to get in the habit of asking on a daily basis. You have much to be grateful for. Find it, and focus on it! Your state will consistently improve and your chances of achieving your goal of straight A's, or any other goal you choose to focus on will increase because of it.

You now have a number of proven tools to work with, and you've seen how they work together to aid you in achieving things that you may not have thought were possible. You've also seen that you only need a few minutes a day to put them into effect. If you are consistent, you will see results right from the start.

Chapter Nine

What to Do
If It All Falls Apart

--Tips for Keeping You on Track

Ok, so it's time to get moving on this stuff. You agree that it's a sound concept, you understand how it works, you've figured out what you want to do, you're excited about the possibilities, you know what to do, and . . . nothing happens! Day after day goes by and you've found one more reason why tomorrow would be the best day to get started. Things come up, all extremely important things to be sure, but when you finally get through with them, you're going to get serious about practicing your new skills. Tomorrow.

What's going on here? If you find yourself stuck in any variation of the above dilemma, you're not alone. Most of us, when embarking on any kind of new project, are bound to run up against that great brake on the wheels of any kind of progress we might desire--*fear*.

Fear: Useful Stuff, But at a High Price

Although sometimes it seems like everyone else is just cruising along untouched while *we* are the only ones affected by fear, the truth is that everyone experiences it. Everyone experiences fear because it's part of our machinery, with a useful purpose. Fear is a survival tool, and a damned good one. But, like any tool, it can

136

be misused. After all, a hammer is a fine tool, after its own fashion, but it might not be the best thing to butter your bread with at dinner. In its intended function, fear helps us survive. But it does so at a price. Our sense of fear alerts us to trouble and prompts us to adopt one of two primary modes: *fight* or *flight*. When we encounter a threatening situation, we either stay and punch it out or we run away, whatever the situation demands. It is fear that triggers the tremendous flow of adrenaline which allows us to perform at levels which we do not usually work from. You've probably heard the story about the mother lifting up a car because her child was trapped underneath. It's rarely that extreme, of course, but fear always accelerates the system's functions. It's like putting double the wattage into a circuit--do it too much and it burns out the system. Fear, while it is helpful when we have our backs against the wall, takes a toll on the body. Our heart rate speeds up, our breathing quickens, and our stress level goes way up.

We Get Too Many Frights From Maybes and Mights

Since there is so much strain placed on the system by fear, it's preferable not to indulge in it unless it's necessary, meaning a *real* threat. But, the truth is that we spend *a lot* of time fearing things that aren't even there. Think about it. How much of what we fear is real? We fear things that *may* take place--if this or that happens first. We spend so much time worrying about things that *might* happen, fearing the *possible* circumstances and the *probable* results. The stuff we spend so much energy worrying about might not even come to pass. "What if I don't pass this test?" "What if I don't get the grades I want?" "What if I don't make the team?" "What if no one asks me to go with them to the prom?" "What if I get caught cheating on this exam?" "What will my parents say when I get home?" "What if my friends find out about . . . ?" I'm sure that if you stopped and thought about it, you could come up with many examples of situations where you spent a good deal of time worrying about something that you were afraid was going to take place and it never did.

These "maybe it will happen" fears wouldn't be that big of a deal *if* the body could tell what's real or not. But, the fact is that it cannot. If fear is triggered, your body reacts *as if* the thing you were afraid of *was* real. It goes through the same strain that it would go through if the situation actually did happen. And this strain drains your body of energy. It makes you tired and unable to put out the necessary effort to succeed. You become anxiety-ridden and stressed out to the point where you cannot function at your best. In fact, you can't even function at your second or third best. Fear saps you. It weakens you and robs you of your purpose.

> A coward dies a thousand deaths,
> A brave man only one.
> --William Shakespeare

Fear Doesn't Help You *Solve* Anything

Now, all of this detriment might be worth putting up with, *if* this state of fear produced results that were helpful in overcoming the situation or condition that was feared. But, on top of the abuse this fear renders on body and mind, *it does nothing to help alleviate the problem*. All it does is put the brakes on the resources you *do* have that would help you solve the problem. And, to further compound the problem, repetition of this action of fearing what "might happen" soon develops into a *habit* of fear. Then, whenever a situation comes up where the outcome is uncertain (which is only about twelve times a day, isn't it?) your chances of accessing this state of fear are very good, and, without even thinking about it, you find yourself apprehensive and, therefore, working from a deficit.

Remember, in its proper capacity, fear serves as a security or alarm system to help you recognize danger. But, like any alarm system, once you are alerted to the danger, you turn off the alarm and *do something* to deal with the situation. The alarm system itself doesn't do anything to work out a solution.

But, when we develop the habit of fear, we are operating with the alarm on much of the time. Imagine how difficult it would be to come up with appropriate or favorable solutions with a car alarm blaring in your ear. Well, it's not that much different with the alarm of fear constantly sounding when you are trying to get things done in your everyday life. Of course, after you get used to it, it doesn't seem so loud, but it *still* stops you from thinking straight.

Fear Controls Your Focus

As if this weren't enough, fear also has another delightful characteristic: It goes a long way towards *helping* you bring about the very condition or situation you fear. It accomplishes this by controlling your focus. Think about it. Let's say there was a big test that you were going to have next week. You have options as to how you could approach it. A good one would be to figure out what was necessary to do in order to prepare for it properly. You could find out what was on it and systematically attack the material with a positive attitude, excited about the challenge of doing well. On the other hand, you could take the more common, fearful approach. The first thing you do is stress out and start complaining to everybody about how you're going to bomb this test that your stupid teacher is going to torture you with. You needn't study that much because you don't have a prayer anyway. As the test date gets nearer, your sense of panic demands that you try to study some, so you hit the books and immediately get confused because you're not exactly sure what to do. After all, you don't have a lot of time and you have other work to do as well. When the day arrives, you're unprepared, you're tired, and you don't feel too well. You spend most of your time staring at stuff you have no idea how to do and, of course, you bomb the thing. Which is just what you were afraid of in the first place, wasn't it?

It all goes back to focus. When you get into a fearful state, what do you focus on? Exactly what you shouldn't, meaning the problem and not the solution. Fear controls your focus. If you are afraid of something, you will spend a lot of time and energy concentrating on it in a negative way. Instead of doing something positive to prepare for doing well, your fear forces you to focus on what can go wrong. And, since you are looking at the negative possibilities with such intensity, your self-talk will certainly begin running your "I'm going to fail, I *know* I'm going to fail" program. This brings in stress, which burns you out and takes away from your ability to work efficiently and effectively. So, in a sense, you become paralyzed and wind up getting the exact results you were afraid of getting.

Replacing the Habit of Fear
With the Habit of Success

It should be painfully clear by now that chronic fear is not your best friend. So, what can you do about it? Well, hopefully, you now have a better understanding of what chronic fear is and how it works against you. While that's not enough to solve the problem, it *is* a sound beginning. Like many things that you fear, fear itself becomes less powerful when it is exposed to the light of understanding. And, as far as the *habit* of fear goes, you've got to realize that it's just like any other habit. If you want to change it, you've got to reprogram it. Fortunately, this book contains several tools which will help you succeed in doing just that. If you consistently work with the information provided for you here, you will begin to see such positive results that much of what you were afraid of will simply lose its hold on you because your newly formed habit of success will *prove* to you that you can indeed accomplish many of the things you were afraid of attempting in the past.

But, like I said at the beginning of the chapter, it is exactly this habit of fear which can so often get in the way of your beginning to seriously work with these techniques. One of the most pervasive fears, and the one that is so effective at short-circuiting our efforts to try anything new or commit to anything which seems difficult at first is the fear of failure.

Fear of Failure

We're all familiar with the fears associated with failure. It's like we don't want to let ourselves down, or set ourselves up for disappointment. All too often, we become afraid of the *possibility* of failure, sometimes so much so that we won't even attempt something. And what do we gain? *Nothing.* Unless you count not having failed as somehow being better than not having attempted something at all. The truth is that the only way to avoid failure completely is to *never do anything.* I'm not exactly sure what the advantage of this particular approach is, however.

> Behold the turtle:
> He only makes progress
> when he sticks his neck out.
> --James Bryant Conant

None of us likes failing, but the real question is: what will we do when we do fail? Most people give up after a failure or two, figuring that they don't have what it takes to succeed. This is wrong thinking. Usually, when we think of great men or women, we tend to assume that their lives are or were an unending series of successes. But, examining their lives usually produces a different picture.

The Road to Success is Lined With Failures

As any successful person will verify, there are numerous failures on the way to success. As an example, just look at baseball. Being a Hall of Famer is certainly a reliable measure of success, isn't it? If a player has a lifetime batting average of .300, it's a safe bet that he is going to wind up in the Hall of Fame. Well, guess what? A .300 hitter *fails* seven times out of ten. That's right, the best hitters in the game *fail* more than twice as many times as they succeed! Another area of greatness is in hitting home runs. If you look at the all-time home run leaders, there's an interesting parallel. Babe Ruth, Reggie Jackson, and Mike Schmidt, to name three of the top ten home run hitters, are also among the all-time leaders in strike-outs. Nobody seems to pay much attention to that, though.

Switching sports, it's important to realize that Fran Tarkenton, the National Football League's all-time leader in pass completions, is the all-time leader in interceptions as well! The point of all of this is that success doesn't come without failure. *You've got to be willing to fail if you want to succeed.*

> The greatest mistake you can make in life
> is to be continually fearing you will make one.
> --Elbert Hubbard

Past Failures Don't Have Anything to Do With the Future

Much of our fear of failure comes from past experience. After all, if you've done poorly at something before, it's easy to doubt that you will be able to do much better in the future. But, in reality, the only power your past performance has on your ability to succeed now is what you *choose* to give it through your limiting beliefs. If you let go of the idea that you can't do it now because you couldn't do it before, you will greatly increase your chances of success. Remember what I've been saying all along: *What you have done in the past has no bearing on what you can do now!*

If at First You Don't Succeed . . .

Business is filled with stories of those who failed often before they finally succeeded. Two of the most famous cases are names that everyone knows: Colonel Sanders and Honda. Colonel Sanders was a retired nobody who wanted to sell a chicken recipe so that he could make more than his social security check would provide. He didn't fail once, twice, or ten times. He failed over a *thousand* times before he finally got someone to buy his recipe! But, when he finally succeeded, he eventually established Kentucky Fried Chicken as one of the most successful fast food chains in the world.

> No great man ever complains of want of opportunity.
> --Ralph Waldo Emerson

Honda, whose name is today associated with one of the more popular lines of cars in the automotive industry, started out as a worker for Toyota before World War II. After numerous setbacks, which included being ridiculed for design ideas, shortages of building materials due to the war, and factories being destroyed by bombs, Honda kept on plugging away until he succeeded in developing the first motorcycle (designed because of a massive gasoline shortage which made cars too expensive to operate. How's that for reframing an obstacle into an opportunity?), and later designing and building his massively successful automotive line.

You know how in cartoons when someone has a great idea, they put a little light bulb above the person's head? Well, Thomas Edison had a great idea about a light bulb. He wanted to *invent* it. Only trouble was, he had a little problem finding the right material to use for the filament, the wire that the electricity passes through inside the bulb. It's said that he tried over *ten thousand* times before he found one that would work properly. When someone asked him how he felt about failing that many times, he told them that far from failing, he had succeeded in finding ten thousand things that would not work!

> A wise man will make more opportunities than he finds.
> --Francis Bacon

As a final example, let's look at the story of another "failure." This gentleman:

☐ had a business venture fail at age 22
☐ lost a legislative race at age 22
☐ had another business venture fail at age 24
☐ had the girl he wanted to marry die when he was 26
☐ suffered severe depression at age 27
☐ failed to win a congressional race at age 34
☐ lost another congressional race at age 36
☐ failed to win a senate race at age 45
☐ failed to obtain the nomination for vice-president at age 47
☐ lost another senate race at age 49

That's a pretty strong list of futility, isn't it? We wouldn't have much cause to remember this man except for one small addition to the list: He was elected president at the age of 52 and went on to become one of the most famous men in world history. Yes, this "failure" is none other than Abraham Lincoln. What would the world have missed out on if *he'd* been deterred by past failures?

Let's Say *You've* Failed a Lot in the Past

Are *you* going to be deterred by past failures? If you are afraid to set goals because you don't think you can achieve them, or you are worried that you cannot achieve the goals you *have* set because you haven't done well in those areas before, remember that where you've been or what you have done before has *no* bearing on what you can do today and tomorrow, *if* you are committed to improving. Look: Maybe you've done poorly in school up to this point and are having trouble seeing yourself doing well. Well, there are some questions you should seriously consider:

☐ What identity were you working with?
☐ What kind of student did you see yourself as?
☐ What beliefs did you chronically program into your brain?
☐ What habits were you stuck in?
☐ How clear was your idea about what you wanted to do?
☐ What kind of focus did you have?
☐ What states did you routinely work from?
☐ What resources did you have access to in order to help you do well?
☐ How fired up were you about doing well?

If you are honest with yourself in answering these questions, you will see that you didn't give yourself half the chance you could have, or didn't put out half the effort you could have, or were flat out working against yourself without even knowing it. Having read this far, you now know about a world of information that you probably didn't know before. Or at least didn't use.

Now, if you've started to work on any of the areas that the above questions touch on, using the techniques provided in this book, don't you think your chances of succeeding are going to improve? Remember, this stuff *works!* So many people have gotten remarkable results in so many different areas of achievement by using this same information. *You* can get similar results in *your* studies and whatever else you choose to turn your attention towards.

If at this point, you *still* don't believe that you can get straight A's. If you're saying to yourself that all of this sounds good for somebody else, but you have been getting F's, or C's, or whatever, and you're just not good enough, or smart enough, you must remember that getting the grades isn't nearly so much a matter of being smart enough as it is a matter of getting rid of the baggage that you've programmed into your mind. Get rid of the negative, disempowering garbage and replace it with the belief that you can do what needs to be done, and you are well on your way to accomplishing your goal. Whatever program you run *consistently,* that is the result you will get. Fortunately, you now know what to do to begin running positive, empowering programs.

What's So Comfortable About the Comfort Zone?

Another sort of fear associated with the inability to really get going with this stuff is the fear of breaking out of your comfort zone, something we are generally resistant to doing. As I said in Chapter Four when discussing goals, our comfort zone is the area of our behavior, whether in thought or action, where we feel comfortable. Comfort zones are based on familiarity. If we are used to something, if a situation or condition holds little in the way of surprises, we tend to be at ease, or comfortable with it.

Now, it is important to understand that comfort zones aren't necessarily made up of things which we would ordinarily associate with comfort. It's quite possible for someone to have a comfort zone consisting of many negative elements. Certainly an extreme example, but one that isn't all that uncommon and should get the point across, is the case of someone who has spent much of his life in prison and who has just gotten out. While locked up, he had a great amount of structure and control placed on him. He was told what to do and when to do it, and he knew exactly what would happen to him if he didn't do it. This life became very routine, and, although it wasn't pleasant, its *familiarity* made it comfortable. In other words, the experience became secure in that it could be relied on. When the convict gets out, all of the structure, the routine, the control, the security is removed. Now the ex-con is on his own in a world which does not provide the security or reliability of the prison environment. And he soon realizes that he cannot cope with it. So, as crazy as it sounds, like many ex-cons in this situation, he winds up doing something that lands him right back in prison, back within the confines of his comfort zone.

Of course, most of us do not have comfort zones that are as severe as the above example, but they *can* be very much like a prison. This is because they are built with limiting ideas, beliefs, and habits, many of which were developed a long time ago and have been unchallenged ever since. So, when something comes along to challenge or attempt to pull us out of our comfort zone, we resist it, fear it, hate it, flee it, or any combination of these. We don't like feeling uncomfortable, so we fight to stay where things are familiar. And the weird thing is, we often do this even if these things are not necessarily what we think we want, and the things that we are resisting will help us get the things we ultimately *do* want. Can you begin to see why you might be having a little trouble getting moving with this stuff? You are at a place right now that, even if you are unhappy with the results this place is getting you, is familiar, and, therefore, comfortable.

If you plan to work at getting new and better results, you will have to break through your comfort zone. Or at least make it much bigger. Don't worry, though, because this is exactly what you *want* to do in order to succeed, and you are in good shape, since you are in possession of a handful of new techniques which are *exactly* what you need in order to get the job done.

The Fear of Being Seen as a Nerd

Sometimes, our identities, or the way we are perceived by others, constitutes a comfort zone which can stifle us in our efforts to improve. Something that frequently happens to students who haven't been successful in the past is that they are afraid to be seen working for good grades because they don't want to look like a nerd or a geek; they don't want to stand out from the crowd. This is a downright sin, folks. The actual number of students who really think in terms of geeks is very small, and it's *not* a club you want to belong to. If you have friends that give you a hard time because you are working to be more successful in school, ask yourself some questions. What are you going to *gain* by being unsuccessful in your schoolwork, especially if you have the capacity to do better? How are you going to benefit by being popular with people who are actively interested in your failure? Do you think they might want you to fail so that *they* won't look bad in comparison? If they *are* going to be against you because you do well, do you really think they are your friends? Regardless of what they do or say concerning your effort to improve your studies, do you actually think they are going to respect you if you screw up when they know you can do better? Why would they? If any one of them felt that *they* could do better, do you think that they would not try to do so?

The crime of this kind of problem is that kids might sometimes make fun of other students they might think of as nerds, but it comes from a defensive stance based in their own insecurity. I've always noticed that regardless of what they said, when it came right down to it, the other students *always* respected the successful students. And I have never seen a student who has been having difficulties who has been given a hard time for doing better. *Never.* The other students generally cheer him or her on because they seem to feel that if it could happen to someone who was having problems like they were, than it just might be possible for *them* as well. So don't let the possible reaction of other students hold you back from getting moving with this stuff. And, if you've had real trouble in the past, don't let the comfort zone of your prior identity get in the way either. The positive feelings you receive from your new successes will more than compensate for any initial discomfort you experience as you break out of your comfort zone.

But What About My Excuses?

Another little comfort zone quirk about getting started on this stuff is best summed up in the statement, "If I do this, I won't have any more excuses for not succeeding." This one's funny because you are happy to have access to this stuff as long as you can keep it at arm's length. You are intrigued by the *possibilities* afforded by these techniques, but you are uncomfortable about the fact of moving on. It's comfortable in your present state, even if this state is not allowing you to produce the results that you want. The fear comes in when you start to realize that access to this stuff *will* allow you to move towards your dreams and goals. It's one thing to be doing less than you want to, and not know why it's happening or not know how to do anything about it. It is quite another to *know* ways to get far greater results. Then, what possible excuse do you have for not achieving those results? This kind of thinking can put undue stress on you and stop you from getting started.

But, it doesn't have to be this way. First of all, *any* degree of work in this direction will bring you some positive results. You get as much out of it as you put into it. Therefore, if you do *any* of this work, you aren't going to fail completely. Of course, there are always possibilities that you might fall down along the way, sometimes to the point of stopping altogether for awhile. Maybe even a long while. But falling down is not failing unless you never get back up.

Coming Back After a Break

Maybe you've already had this happen to you and are just getting back to it after a break and are reading this chapter again, or are reading the whole book again in order to get help in starting over. Well, so what if you are starting over? You fall down, you get up. Congratulations for starting over! I won't bore you with how many times I had to start over, even with writing this book. Life is made up of a series of starting overs. It doesn't make any difference how many times it takes you to get it right because success is a *process*, not a destination. The true progress that you get, the real benefit that comes from your doing this, is not what you get in the way of stuff, but what you *become* through your achievements.

It's like hard work. The great thing about learning to work hard isn't the fruits that hard work brings you, but in the way that you feel, the *state* you are in while working hard. If you doubt this, look at all of the successful people who are known for their work habits. Do they quit working hard after they become successful enough to live comfortably without any extra work? We always hear people say that they would retire and do nothing if they suddenly became successful, but the ones who actually do become successful never seem to just retire. They know that the *process* is the key, not the stuff it brings.

And, speaking of hard work, it is just the stuff that another one of our possible fears is made of.

Working Smarter, Not Harder

Are you worried that this whole endeavor is going to mean too much work and extra effort for you? If you are, stop for a second and think. It's not a matter of working harder. It's a matter of working smarter, of working more *efficiently* and *focusing* in order to get the results that you want. You're using the same energy that you were using before, but you are aiming it all in the same direction, instead of throwing it all over the place. There's something called *drag energy*. It's the amount of effort needed to resist something or to stop something from happening, like brakes do on your bicycle. By eliminating the resistance that used to hold back your efforts in the past, you free up a lot of energy to be used positively towards your new goals. Ask anybody who is successfully involved in a project or endeavor and they will tell you that the more they get into it, the less tired they feel.

> The greater the will,
> the greater the flow of energy.
> --Paramahansa Yogananda

The drag energy of resistance takes far more out of you than positive hard work does because it stops all momentum. When you are moving ahead willingly, you develop momentum and it takes far less energy to *keep* going than it takes to *get* going. It's like riding a bike. Doesn't it take much more effort to reach your maximum speed than it does to keep going at maximum speed once you achieve it? Once you get momentum, you've won half the battle. So don't worry that achieving far greater levels of success than you are used to will require far greater effort than you have expended in order to achieve your less than successful results. Remember, it's working smarter, not harder.

If I Do It Once, I'll Always Have to Do It

Along the same lines, there is a frequently expressed objection to getting involved in a success program like this which is: "If I succeed, people will always expect me to do it, and I will always have to achieve these kinds of results. This will make me have to work harder all the time." This fear seems to come from the pressure that a lot of students feel from parents and teachers and other folks who they think expect too much from them. But, this is really just a matter of not realizing who is really keeping score and having a little trouble with our old friend, the comfort zone.

It's understandable that students would feel the pressure of expectations. After all, it *is* there. The only problem here is in the perception that students have concerning where the pressure is coming from. Think of it this way. Let's say that you worked at this stuff for a while and succeeded at getting straight A's for a quarter or semester. Now, do you think that you are going to want to go back to your old ways of getting B's, or C's, or D's, or whatever? After all of the pleasure you received from getting the A's?

Believe me, I've been on both sides of this fence. I got rotten grades in high school and I've gotten straight A's in college. There is no pressure or expectation from *anyone* that could have had nearly as much influence on my behavior as succeeding at getting the A's did. I had *no* desire to get the rotten grades again, and the effort it would have taken me in drag energy to fall back to that level would have been far more exhausting than whatever I was putting out to maintain my A's.

You don't have to worry about other people's expectations. Success is *far* more fun than failure. Once you get a taste of it, you will be happy to maintain it and your enthusiasm towards doing so will be far more than enough to keep you going in the right direction.

Self-Sabotage: Losing the Whole Because of a Part
Unless, of course, you self-sabotage. Self-sabotage, or undermining yourself, is an ugly idea, but it happens quite frequently as people begin to succeed. It goes back to the comfort zone. Many of us have learned to see ourselves belonging within certain limits or deserving only so much because of actions other people have taken or things they have said about us. Haven't we all had the delightful experience when we were little (or maybe not so little), of some teacher, parent, or friend telling us that we were stupid or lazy or bad or whatever, when they were angry with us? Because we believed them, their limited perceptions or beliefs about us became *our* limiting perceptions or beliefs. Now, once we begin to move away from these limits, it is quite possible that we might get uncomfortable and start behaving in ways that would ensure that we get back into our comfort zone.

Self-sabotage happens because *some part* of the results you desire bothers you and your brain is trying to help you avoid it. The problem is that by avoiding the part, you lose out on all of the rest of the successful stuff you *do* want.

Find Out Why the Sabotage Doesn't Make Sense
When examined, many of the reasons why we self-sabotage don't make a whole lot of sense. But when has *that* stopped us from

doing something? Luckily, once you see self-sabotage for what it is, it gets much easier to work it out and keep moving in the direction you want to go.

Even more fortunate for you is that much of what goes into self-sabotage has already been touched on here. For example, say you get excited about the possibilities of really getting moving on this stuff. But, on some level, you are afraid that it is going to take too much effort to do well, so you don't follow through. Well, now you have a better idea about how succeeding means working smarter, not harder. As you become more comfortable with this new idea (and, yes, programming it in as a new belief is an excellent way to do it), the sabotage that may have been troubling you in the past will lose its grip and you won't have to fight it as much.

Similarly, another self-sabotage problem is that people start to succeed and begin to feel uncomfortable with their success because they haven't done anything like this before. So they don't feel they deserve it, or even worse, they feel that this isn't *them*, and they are faking it somehow. Soon, other people will catch on and they will be seen as the fakes they are. Therefore, in order to stop this process of getting caught, they pull the plug on their efforts and get back to where it's comfortable--in their comfort zone.

Again, you now have more insight into this little demon. First of all, your efforts as well as your results in the past have nothing to do with the present or future. If you change your strategies and your habits into ones which have proven successful for other people, you too will get similar results. Who cares what you could or couldn't do before? Hey, when I was a baby I couldn't even *walk*. Now I hardly even have to think about it! If your identity changes, *you* change. Do you think you were faking it when you learned how to ride a bike? Believe me, you didn't know how to do it before that first time. Do you remember your parents or any of your friends saying, "Hey, who do you think you are riding that bike like that? You can't *really* ride it. Get off it and go back to walking like you should be doing, you big fake!" As a matter of fact, if you were the first one to successfully learn to ride, you can be sure that your friends wanted to be just like you. So what's different now? If you haven't been successful in the past, it makes no difference whatsoever. You didn't know how to ride a bike, you learned to ride a bike. You didn't know how to be a successful student, you learn how to be a successful student. No one is going to think you are a fake or think that you don't deserve it. At least no one worth listening to. (Please know that 99% of the time that someone is getting down on someone else's success or achievement, the real reason is that they are trying to compensate for their own feelings of inadequacy.)

Weeding Out Self-Sabotage

And so it goes with any self-sabotaging issue. Once you know this stuff, it's much easier to deal with the self-sabotaging issues that come up from time to time. First, find out what you are trying to avoid. Then, examine it to see why you might *want* to avoid it. (This would be secondary gain.) If you can spot an error in reasoning, this will begin to weaken the self-sabotaging tendency's power because it won't be able to go by unquestioned any longer. But, this is only a beginning. You know by now that it doesn't make any difference if a disempowering belief makes sense or not. If it's programmed into your computer, your brain is going to run it. What you do is recognize it so that you can begin changing the program. With all of your new information and tools, you can now do this much easier than you ever could before. *If* you get working on it.

Please Don't Start *Trying* Now

Well, now that you have a better understanding of how fears can keep you from getting going, this would seem to be the perfect time for me to encourage you to take this material and try hard to reach the goals you have set for yourself. But I'm not going to do it. I am not going to tell you to *try*. It might sound strange, but if you try, you will probably *not* succeed. This is an important concept to grab hold of, and it is one that often meets resistance.

(Of course, this doesn't mean that try *always* means fail. Words have different meanings and usages for different situations, and the brain, being the sophisticated piece of work that it is, can tell the difference. Obviously, when you use the word try in any of its other meanings, such as trying a new recipe or trying out for a team or something, your brain isn't going to interpret it as failing. When I speak of trying in this context, however, I mean in the sense of attempting to accomplish something. These are the instances when it can easily become a code for failure.)

So often we are told to try. "Give it a try." "Try harder." "All you have to do is try." On the surface, these encouragements sound like good advice, since trying sounds like a positive thing to do. But "trying" contains built-in failure because deep in the subconscious, where the brain conducts the large part of its business, "try" means the same thing as "fail."

> Do or do not.
> There is no try.
> --Yoda

Well, at Least I Failed

This idea sounds crazy at first, but think about it. When someone gets in a situation where they do not succeed, what is the first thing that they say? "Well, at least I tried." And, maybe they did. But listen closely to what is really happening down at the bottom, where your programs are. If you fail at something and say that you tried, or you have someone telling you that it's ok because "at least you tried," it becomes an *excuse* for your failure. Whether it's a good excuse or a bad excuse doesn't matter at all. It's still an excuse, something designed to get you off the hook for failing. Now, if every time you fall short on a goal or project or assignment or test or whatever, you fall back on the excuse "Well, at least I tried," then your brain begins to link the two ideas together. Once this link is established (and it doesn't take very long), every time you say "I'll try," your brain hears *"try"* and, because of past experience, joins it with *"fail."* Therefore, when you say "I'll try," you are sending your brain the subtle message that you don't expect to succeed, and your brain will accommodate you.

Take This Little Test

If you don't think this is true, put yourself to a little test. The next time you find yourself in a situation where you say "I will try," stop and say "I will do it" instead. If you get a feeling like jelly in your belly, a feeling like you aren't *really* comfortable with the commitment, know that you have set yourself up to fall short. You might come close, but you probably won't make it the whole way. Think about it. What were you after when you first stated your intention? Did you really think you would succeed? If you did, then you wouldn't have any trouble saying "I will do it," as opposed to "I will *try*." If you do have trouble saying "I will do it," then somewhere deep down, you don't feel like you will get the job done. On some level, there's a basic lack of confidence. And that's all it takes. For, as you've learned by now, you are going to produce results consistent with your beliefs. And your beliefs are not as confident as you are pretending to be. *Try,* no matter how close you come, means *fail.* Remember, you have a great interest in being right, and your brain will guide you towards the result you *believe* you should get. If your brain is set up to interpret "try" as "fail," then your efforts will guide you in that direction. Even if you're not paying attention and are thinking you *might* succeed this time.

I'll *Try* to Call You

Another reason why trying leads to *not* succeeding is that we quite often use "I'll try" when we secretly have no intention of doing something. You know how it works. Someone asks you to do something and you don't really want to, but you can't get out of it gracefully. What do you tell them? "Well, I'll try . . . " "I'll try and get back to you on that." "I'll try and get it done." "I'll try to be back by then." "I'll try to get in touch with her." "I'll try harder next time." Now, you know you're not *really* going to do it when you say it, and so does your brain. So, when you say it to *yourself*, your brain doesn't take *you* any more seriously than it does when you say it to someone else. It knows better. It hears the same message: "I'm not going to do it."

Don't Try to Do It. *Expect* to Do It!

So what are you going to do? Are you at the mercy of "I'll try"? Of course not! But, if you've been accustomed to saying "I'll try," or using "at least I tried" as an excuse, then you will have to do some programming. The nice thing is that, by now, you already know how to do this. It shouldn't be that big of a deal. Here's what you do. From now on, you *must* get in the habit of saying "I'll do it" instead of "I'll try." Now, maybe it doesn't sound like that much of a difference, but it is. Think of it this way. Do you think for a moment that when Barry Bonds goes up to the plate with the bases loaded that he is "trying" to get a hit? No no no no no. Barry Bonds walks up to the plate with every intention of getting a hit. No matter how many times he doesn't come through, he *still* goes up there knowing that he is going to get a hit *this* time.

Of course, he is not alone. Charles Barkley, the perennial NBA all-star, has said that when the game is on the line and there is one final shot to be made, *he* wants the ball. And, he *expects* to make that last shot *every single time*. So, he gets the ball in that situation. And sometimes he doesn't make the shot. But it makes no difference whatsoever to Sir Charles. When the time comes, he *still* expects to make the shot, and he *still* gets the ball. And, even though he sometimes misses the shot, he often makes it. And that makes all the difference. He knows that he is *the* guy to go to, and he knows that in the same situation, many, if not most of the players in the NBA, *don't* want the ball. Sure, they might *try* to make the shot if it came to that, but they don't really expect to make it.

Again, it's not just in sports that this stuff is exhibited. Successful people in all walks learn to focus on *doing* instead of trying to do. It's an attitude. A major difference between the successful person and the unsuccessful one is that the successful person goes into each new situation *expecting* to succeed right away, while the unsuccessful person generally feels that he or she will fail at first. Certainly, since I have already said that the successful person will often fail along the way to success, I am not implying that success is automatic just because it is expected. But the *expectation* of success goes a long way towards speeding up the process, or improving the chances of success. If there are failures along the way, however, the successful person doesn't dwell on them. He or she just focuses on the positive elements, learns what there is to learn and moves on, expecting to succeed the next time. The unsuccessful person, on the other hand, will dwell on the failures, ignoring the positive aspects, and assume that they are destined to fail, thereby giving up.

> Though he fail many times, the man who keeps on striving,
> who is undefeated within, is truly a victorious person.
> No matter how many times you fall down,
> get up with a determination to be victorious.
> --Paramahansa Yogananda

Knowledge Is Not Power

There's a saying that knowledge is power. It sounds good, but it *isn't* true. Many people have the knowledge and, sad to say, they haven't become any more successful because of this knowledge because *having* it was *not* enough. In fact, many of the students who read this book will *not* succeed either. That's right. Despite having access to the very techniques that thousands of people have used very successfully, they will *still* fail. They will fail because they will not *do* anything with the information that they have been given. They will not *receive* it. Imagine that. It's like wanting to get into a locked room and not using the key that has been given to you to open the door. It sounds insane that someone would not use these keys to success, but it's all too true.

Every year, thousands of books are sold which contain techniques such as these. Every year, thousands of people attend seminars, classes, and workshops (at great expense) to learn this same information in one form or another. And, sad to say, they never *do* anything with the knowledge. Knowledge is *not* power. *Action*, based on that knowledge, *is*. You have now completed the first step. You have the knowledge needed to obtain great success in your studies and anything else you choose to pursue. Whether you will be one of the many people who will wait until "someday" to put it to use, or you will be one of the ones who will begin succeeding today, only you know. I have given you some very effective keys, but *you* have to unlock the door. Do it! Please, please, please, do it.

Index

Excuses
    trying and 155
    comfort zone and 148
    for not doing the job 83
Expectation
    key to identity 10
    increases success 157-158
    instead of trying 157
    vs. wanting 10-11

F
Fear
    controls focus 139-140
    solves nothing 138-139
    high price of 136-137
    of being a nerd 147-148
    of change 4
    of failure 4, 141-142
    replacing habit of 140
    why nothing happens 136
Focus
    aim RAS positively 77
    and fear 139-140
    definition of 67
    for fun 74-75
    link to goals 73-74
    negative results
        from 68-69
    being positive
        isn't faking 72-73
    problem of poor focus 4
    quality of life
        determined by 67
    review with
        straight A's 124-127

Focus (cont.)
    trained for negative 69-70
    use your RAS 75-77
    you get what you
        focus on 70
Ford, Henry 30, 61

G
Gasset, Ortega Y 65
Gide, Andre 43
Gilbert, Dr. Robert 36
Goals
    1953 Yale study of 44
    aid in motivation 47
    know when you've
        reached it 57-58
    desire to keep vague 42
    guidelines for setting
        51-62
    have a timeline 59-61
    make work fun 47-50
    momentum created 51
    moving past distractions
        and obstacles 45-47
    overcoming comfort
        zone 50-51
    provide direction 43-44
    push ahead even
        if unsure 61-62
    review with
        straight A's 113-116
    risk involved 43
    size of goal
        not important 49

Joubert, Joseph 73

K
King, Basil 76
Knowledge
  is not power 159

L
Lincoln, Abraham 14

M
Mallarme, Stephane 40
Marden, Orison Swett 49
Mill, John Stuart 18
Momentum
  and drag energy 151
  and imaging 41
  goals help maintain 51

N
Neural pathways 24, 40
  shoe-tying example
   24-25
Nicklaus, Jack 33
Nietzsche, Friedrich 84

P
Past performance vs. future
  22-23, 30, 35, 142, 152
Plato 96
Posture (State part one)
  effect on state 81-82

Posture (cont.)
  helps create state 84
  primary and secondary
   gain 82-83
  review with
   straight A's 127-130
  use posture "as if" 89-90
  using for energy and
   enthusiasm 85, 88-91
  which state is real 87-88

R
Reality
  and self-talk 92-93
  beliefs filter out 28
  everything in "real" world
   imagined first 36
  and reframing 100-101
  vs. beliefs 19
  which state is real 87-88
  why is realism always
   negative 35-36, 71
Reframing (State part two)
  and mistakes 102-103
  and reality 100-101
  review with
   straight A's 133-134
Reticular Activating
  System (RAS) 75-77, 126
Retton, Mary Lou 33
Russell, Bill 33
Ruth, G.H. (Babe) 142

About the Author

Frederick Hageman teaches English at Northgate High School in Walnut Creek, a suburb of San Francisco. Having received many accolades from students and parents, as well as excellent evaluations from administrators, he wondered why, while doing so well on one hand, he felt that he was failing to reach many of the kids in his classes. Realizing that something was amiss beyond the usual woes of education, he set upon his present course of working to fix the students instead of worrying about fixing the schools. Out of his work with individuals and informal classes dealing with the problems that students face comes *Making the Grades*.

Mr. Hageman has been on both sides of the fence in his school experience and understands the challenges with which students must cope. An admittedly awful student during his own school years, he received poor grades and barely graduated high school. After suffering through one dead end job after another, he began college at the age of twenty-six and went on to graduate with top honors. Having experienced and surmounted many of the same difficulties that routinely challenge students, he is committed to helping them overcome these difficulties so that they, too, might move on to success.

Order Form

To order additional copies of *Making the Grades*, send this form
or a copy plus a check or money order for $14.95 each to:

Making the Grades
Rising Crescent Publishing
P.O. Box 7703-A
Berkeley, CA 94707-0703

Please add $2.50 for first book and 75 cents for each additional
book for shipping. Please allow three to four weeks for delivery.

California residents please add 8.25% or applicable sales tax.

Name _____ Phone (___) _____

Address _____

City _____ State _____ Zip _____

Quantity discounts are available. Please write to the publisher for
details.